EARTH HEALING MEDITATIONS

GUIDED IMAGERY FOR GROUPS

HELEN JOY BUCK

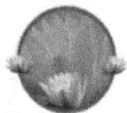

www.thefloatinglily.com.au

ISBN 978-0-9807708-3-4   2nd edition

Earth Healing Meditations Guided Imagery for Groups
1st edition © 2010 Helen Joy Buck

Cover Art and Logo by Leanne M Williams,
Diamond Light Graphic Design and Spiritual Artist.
Front cover photo taken by Russell and Vicki Medway.

National Library of Australia Cataloguing-in-Publication entry
Creator: Buck, Helen Joy, author.
Title: Earth healing meditations : guided imagery for groups / Helen Joy Buck.
Edition: Second edition
ISBN: 9780980770834 (paperback)
Notes: Includes bibliographical references.
Subjects: Meditation.
Spiritual life.
Dewey Number: 158.12

To Mother Earth and her inhabitants

Contents

PRELUDE

Earth Healing Meditations has been designed as a resource for those wanting to hold guided imagery meditation groups. This book explains step-by-step procedures on how to set up a meditation group. This includes instructions on how to energetically prepare, with good clearing and protection steps.

Meditation is a truly wonderful way to relax, which has many health benefits for those who meditate regularly. *Earth Healing Meditations* takes things a little further, benefiting both the meditater and the Earth.

With forty one guided imagery scripts to choose from you are sure to enjoy *Earth Healing Meditations.*

HOW TO USE THIS BOOK

When holding a meditation group the preparation steps are important. It is essential not to skip this section no matter how eager you are to get started.

The following steps explain this book's meditation format.

EXPECTATIONS

If running a meditation group or meditating for the first time, participants will want to know what to expect. Meditation experiences vary with each individual and experiences usually change as the participant becomes more adept at the process. Some participants go to a blank, still space and do not recall the group leader reading the meditation script or the music that is played in the background. This state is not to be confused with sleep. Some participants will see pictures in their mind's eye during the meditative state. Sometimes these pictures are in colour while other times they are not. Some will think the meditation with their thought processes. Others will perceive feelings or perhaps pleasant fragrances during the meditation. Other participants will follow the script to the letter while others go on their own version of the read script. Some participants will come out of the meditation and open their eyes easily, while others will need a little more time to come out of the meditation state. All of these responses are fine and normal.

It is recommended that the group leader mention to each participant that they are in complete control throughout the meditation, and that they can open their eyes and sit out of the meditation if they feel uncomfortable at any time. Discuss the possible range of experiences with the meditation group prior to starting. It should be explained to the meditation participants that if any imagery has a negative connotation to them then all they need to do is simply change that image to something they are comfortable with.

When meditating for the first time it may take a little while to settle into the desired state. It is usual for thoughts of the day to flitter through your mind when you first start practising. Meditating becomes easier the more you do it.

Depending on the size of the meditation room and the size of the group, the meditations may be done seated and in a circle or, if space allows, some may like to lie down. It is better if participants do not cross their arms or legs, so as not to restrict the flow of energy around the body. It is important to feel physically comfortable. Having a box of tissues available can be useful, in case participants need to cough or sneeze during the meditation. Remind participants to turn off their mobile phones or cell phones and to go to the toilet prior to the meditation session.

CREATING A CLEAR AND PROTECTED ENVIRONMENT

When holding meditation groups, you need to provide an energetically clear room in which to meditate. Participants should also be energetically clear. An environment should be cleared of e.g. passed over spirits, which I refer to as 'pass-overs', 'step-ins' and 'step-outs'.

'Pass-overs' are spirits who have passed, but haven't passed to the Light of Higher levels. Sometimes a Spirit that has left the body will feel the lack of the body and be loath to leave the physical plane behind, so the Spirit will 'step-in' to the auric pattern of an unprotected person, and then 'step out' while they are protected.

Excess colour, sound, fragrance and emotion can be cleared, as these things can be seen as negative to the auric pattern of a room or person. After the environment has been cleared it must then be protected. Clearing is necessary first, followed by protection, as you don't want to protect or close in the negativity. A variety of clearing and protecting methods will be explained.

I cannot emphasise enough the importance of clearing and protecting before meditating, whether meditating on your own or when running a meditation group. Clearing and protecting is important to set a safe environment for yourself and the group. This is necessary as you will be unaware of what type of day your group members have had, who they have met during the day and what energies they have come into contact with. To begin without clear and protected auric patterns could be inviting trouble. Best to clear and protect so you are all in an appropriate and safe environment to begin the meditation.

There are many ways to clear and protect, and it is not so important how it is done, as long as it is done. So before you open up in a spiritual way, as you do when meditating, it is always wise to clear and protect the room you will be meditating in, yourself, and those participating in the meditation group. Here are some suggestions on how to clear and protect.

METHODS OF CLEARING AND PROTECTING

(1) Sage or smudge sticks from the Native American culture can be used to clear negative energy from a person's auric pattern and your meditation room. Light the sage or smudge stick and then gently blow it out so that it smoulders, creating a fragrant smoke. This sage smoke is then swept through the person's auric pattern with your hand or a feather.

When clearing a room with the sage smoke, work your way around the room while holding the smouldering smudge stick. Sweep the smoke throughout the air, concentrating on the corners of the room, doorways and windows. Hold the intention that all forms of negativity are raised up and bound to the White Light in the name of the Creator/Great Spirit/God/Goddess/Lord Buddha/all that is good, etc. The intent is important because if you don't bind it to the White Light then the negative energy is free to re-connect with your auric pattern or someone else's.

(2) Tibetan singing bowls can be used to clear negative energy from your meditation room. Tibetan singing bowls are rung using a wooden beater or they can be struck with a wooden beater to release their sound. To clear a room with a Tibetan singing bowl, strike it with a wooden beater to release the sound and then move the bowl around the walls of the room, concentrating on the corners of the room doorways and windows, once again holding the intention to clear all forms of negativity, raising it up and binding it to the White Light in the name of the Creator/Great Spirit/God/Goddess/Lord Buddha/all that is good, etc.

(3) Space Clearing Skin and Space Mist is a truly beautiful spray, which uses the properties of *Australian Bush Flower Essences* to create sacred, safe and harmonious environments. It clears negativity and purifies and releases negative emotional, mental and psychic energies. Spray the mist throughout your meditation room and through the person's auric pattern, which you are clearing. It is produced by Ian White the founder of *Australian Bush Flower Essences.*
Available from: www.ausflowers.com.au

(4) Words or Prayer can be used to clear auric patterns and evoke protection. Clearing and protecting words that I like to use are adapted from *Chiron Healing®*

Examples:

'I now clear everything negative including pass-overs, step-ins and step-outs affecting [insert group leader's name] raise it up and bind it to the Divine Light in the name of [insert your belief system i.e. Creator/Great Spirit/ God/Goddess/Lord Buddha/all that is good, etc.]'

'I now clothe myself in a robe of White Light for my protection.' OR 'I now clothe myself in a robe of White Light composed of the love, power and wisdom of God not only for my own protection but so that all those who see it and come in contact with it are drawn to God and are healed.' (Isobel M. Hickey, *'It Is All Right.'*)

'I surround myself in a strong protective Silver Bubble and ask that this Silver Bubble be connected to [insert your belief system i.e. Creator/Great Spirit/God/Goddess/Lord Buddha/all that is good, etc.]'

(5) Visualisations can achieve a similar effect. You could do something similar by visualising White Light washing up from under your feet, washing anything that is not of the Light up and away up from your body and its proximity, binding it to the White Light high above your head. Then see a bright White Light streaming down, surrounding and protecting your whole body. Finally see yourself surrounded in a Silver Bubble and see the Silver Bubble connected to your Creator, to your belief system.

(6) A Chiron Healing® Burning Dish with dedicated candles work extremely well for clearing negative energies that affect people and rooms. With this method you can clear the meditation room, yourself and those that have booked in to attend the meditation group prior to them arriving.

Used with candles dedicated to the Light, protection symbols and 'fire as nature's cleanser' it makes a worthwhile purchase to assist in maintaining clear energy fields.

Available from www.chariclo.com

HOW TO USE A CHIRON HEALING®
BURNING DISH FOR CLEARING
NEGATIVE ENERGIES

1. Dedicate three white candles to the Light i.e. leave in a Holy Book, such as the Bible, overnight, then say a dedication or blessing such as the Lord's Prayer to align them with 'good'.

2. On a piece of white paper write the words for clearing negative energies that feel right for you. Something like 'I now burn and clear everything negative, including pass-overs, step-ins and step outs affecting [insert the person or peoples' names or the address of premises, for example - your name, the meditation room and the names of those attending the meditation group] raise it up and bind it to the Light in the name of [insert your belief system i.e. Creator/Great Spirit/ God/Goddess/Lord Buddha/all that is good, etc.]' Underneath that, write the three symbols of protection - the rune of protection, the infinity sign and the balanced cross.

ᛉ   ∞   +

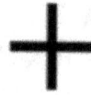

3. Fold your paper in half and then in half again, so that the creases form a cross.

4. Light the three candles and ignite your folded paper from all three candles, making certain that all of the paper burns. You may need to move it with a wooden match or skewer, or drip wax on it to make sure that all the paper burns. Do not use a metal skewer as this can bind the negativity to you, the exact opposite to what you want.

5. Now follow with protection by visualising whoever has just been cleared of negative energies, for example - you, the meditation room and those participants attending the meditation group, surrounded in White Light and then surrounded in a Silver Bubble which is connected up to your Creator -Source of energy.

Whichever clearing method(s) you choose to use, it is essential to follow with protection by simply visualising those you have just cleared surrounded in protective White Light and then a Silver Bubble around that. See the Silver Bubble connected up to your Creator - Source of energy. White Light is used for protection as it contains all the colours of the Light spectrum and the Silver Bubble acts as a protective shell.

The group leader of the meditation group needs to do these clearing and protection steps not only for themselves but for the meditation room as part of the preparation procedures prior to every meditation group held. A clearing and protection visualisation has been built into the meditation introduction for the group participants. Preferably clearing and protection steps should also occur for the meditation participants prior to meditating.

After using your chosen clearing and protection method(s) for the meditation room, reinforce the process by stating aloud or in your mind:

'I now clear everything negative, including pass-overs, step-ins and step-outs affecting this meditation room, raise it up and bind it to the Light in the name of the Creator. I ask that the meditation room be protected in Love and Light, so that only those walking the path of Light may enter. I ask that three tall etheric candles be placed in the room and that guardian angels and guides stand in each corner of the room to guide and protect all those participating in the meditation group.'

Remember always to ask for assistance from your Creator/ Great Spirit/God/Goddess/Lord Buddha/all that is good, etc. For example, 'I mentally request assistance from the Creator, Ascended Masters, Angels and Guides for protection, safety and guidance of the meditation group'.

You may like to ask them to stand guard in the corners of the room for the duration of your meditation, if it fits with your belief system.

Once you have created the clear and protected environment it is recommended that the meditation participants remain seated in the protected circle until the completion of the meditation session.

MEDITATION INTRODUCTION

When ready to start, dim the lighting, play soft relaxation music in the background and read the meditation introduction in a calming and gentle voice. The meditation introduction allows the participants to begin to relax and prepare to enter the meditative state. It includes a clearing and protection visualisation.

MEDITATION SCRIPT

Following the meditation introduction, continue reading the chosen meditation script in a calming and gentle voice. You have a variety of meditation scripts to choose from. It is best to decide upon and familiarise yourself with the appropriate meditation script before beginning.

MEDITATION ENDING

After reading the meditation script in a calming and gentle voice, follow by reading the meditation ending. The meditation ending allows enough time for the participants to return from their meditative state. This should be read slowly and in a slightly louder voice.

Some participants will come out of the meditative state more quickly than others. You may need to read the meditation ending again for some, allow them the time needed to come out of the meditative state. Once all meditators have opened their eyes, give them a few moments to contemplate their experience. Increase the intensity of the lighting in the room and allow everyone a moment to stretch a little and move their limbs.

At the end of the meditation the group leader will need to check on all participants by asking them if they feel they are fully present in their physical body. Some participants may need to stretch for a little longer to focus on their physical body.

Some of the participants will like to discuss and share their meditation experience, others will not. This decision should be respected. Remember that everyone's meditation experience is his or her own and that meditation is certainly not a competition. As meditative states vary there is value in learning how others perceive theirs.

CLOSING DOWN

When opening up in a spiritual way, as you do automatically when you meditate, it is important to close down afterwards. It is not wise to be left open in inappropriate circumstances. So make time to clear and protect again, as described earlier in Words or Prayer or Visualisation and then close down by making the sign of a cross over the third eye three times, once for each level of consciousness, or do a clockwise sealing motion with your right hand over the third eye.

Then close the 'feeling centre', which is the 'diamond' shaped area in the stomach, solar plexus and upper reproductive area, which receives the energy of every thought, word or problem received from the outside world. This is the place where 'gut instinct' and 'hunches' are gathered.

To close down the feeling centre, extend your arms left and right from the sides of your body and imagine that you are gathering threads and drawing them together in a bundle in front of your Feeling Centre. With your right (physical) hand closest to your body and your left (spiritual) hand over the top, bring your hands together as though you were cutting these threads between your closed hands. Close them right off - and open your hands a little so that you have a small gap - about the size of a ten-cent piece. Then imagine White Light coming out of your right hand as you move your hand in a clockwise sealing motion up the centre of your body from your feet to above your head to seal any leaks of energy from your chakras. (*Chiron Healing®*)

Now that you have ensured everyone, including yourself, is cleared, protected and closed down, you can rest assured that you have done your best to ensure the meditation participants are in the right state to have a restful sleep or continue with the rest of their day.

Mentally send the three etheric candles back that you set up in the room and say thank you to your Creator, Angels, Ascended Masters and Guides.

You have just run a successful meditation group. Well done!

MEDITATION FORMAT SUMMARY

Step 1.

Clear and protect yourself, the room you are going to be meditating in and the meditation group participants.

Step 2.

Briefly answer any questions the meditation participants may have in regards to their expectations of the meditation process. Then instruct those that will be meditating to take a comfortable position seated or lying down, eyes closed with their arms and legs uncrossed. Dim the lighting and play soft relaxation music in the background during the meditation.

Step 3.

In a slow gentle voice read the Meditation Introduction to the meditation group.

Step 4.

In a slow and gentle voice read one of the Meditation Scripts to the meditation group.

Step 5.

In a slow but slightly louder voice read the Meditation Ending to the meditation group.

Step 6.

Participants may like to share their meditation experience with the others in the meditation group.

Step 7.

The group leader and participants should then clear and protect with words/prayer or visualisation and close down.

MEDITATION
INTRODUCTION

Closing your eyes... and taking a deep breath.

Just relaxing... and resting... as you listen to my voice... and take note of where you are... allowing my voice to guide you... during this meditation.

Knowing that you are safe... and that you are in control... during this meditation.

Firstly, visualise... your aura being cleansed... and cleared of everything negative.

In your mind... asking for Divine assistance during the meditation... while all negativity is raised up... and bound to the biggest... brightest... White Light.

To be taken care of... by your Creator/Great Spirit/ God/Goddess/Lord Buddha/ and all that is good.

(Short Pause)

Breathing deeply... release the stressors of the day.

(Long Pause)

Breathing deeply... relax your body.

(Long Pause)

Breathing deeply... at your own pace.

(Long Pause)

Breathing in... and breathing out.
Release the stressors from the day... ask for Divine assistance...while all negativity is raised up... and bound to the biggest... brightest... White Light.
To be taken care of by your Creator/Great Spirit/ God/Goddess/Lord Buddha/and all that is good.

(Pause)

14

Now surround yourself in protective White Light... made up of the Love of the universe...

(Short Pause)

And then surround yourself in a Silver Bubble... that is connected up to your Creator... to your belief system.

(Short Pause)

Protected... safe... and guided always.

MEDITATION ENDING

Breathing deeply.

You feel at peace.

Breathing deeply... focus on your physical body.

(Pause)

In the centre of your being now... as you breathe deeply.

Filling your lungs with universal energy... and your feet with the grounding energy from Mother Earth.

(Long Pause)

In the very centre of your being now... as you focus your attention on your physical body.

(Pause)

Breathing deeply... fill your lungs with universal energy and your feet, legs and body with the grounding energy from Mother Earth.

(Pause)

You are in the very centre of your being now... aware of your physical body.

Filling your entire physical body.

(Long Pause)

You are now focused on your physical body... from the tips of your fingers... to the tips of your toes... your whole body... filling your entire physical body.

In the very centre of your being now... filling your entire physical body.

(Long Pause)

Now in your physical body... you feel re-energised... and you begin to stretch.
Moving your fingers and your toes.

Aware of your physical body... and your physical-ness.
You move your arms and your legs... stretching your body now.

(Long Pause)

Focused and centred in your physical body.
Re-energised... centred... and grounded.
You take 3 deep breaths... and open your eyes.

(Short Pause)

You open your eyes now.

MEDITATION SCRIPTS

LOVING AND APPRECIATING MOTHER EARTH: HARMONIC EARTH CONDITIONS

Just breathing... at your own pace... and picturing the Mother Earth.
Loving... and appreciating her... and smiling with her.
Spending time with her.

And the moon glows... and shines luminously upon the earth... and you embrace it... love it... respect it... and treasure its presence and role in our existence.

(Short Pause)

And the moon smiles.
Harmonic Earth conditions.

Just breathing... at your own pace... and picturing the Mother Earth.
Loving... and appreciating her... and smiling with her.
Spending time with her.

And the wind blows across the land... and you embrace it... love it... respect it... and treasure its presence and role in our existence.

(Short Pause)

And the wind smiles.
Harmonic Earth conditions.

Just breathing... at your own pace... and picturing the Mother
Earth.
Loving... and appreciating her... and smiling with her.
Spending time with her.

And the frost freezes... and coats the land... and you embrace
it... love it... respect it... and treasure its presence and role in
our existence.

(Short Pause)

And the frost smiles.
Harmonic Earth conditions.

Just breathing... at your own pace... and picturing the Mother
Earth.
Loving... and appreciating her... and smiling with her.
Spending time with her.

And the snow falls gently... layering itself against the land...
and you embrace it... love it... respect it... and treasure its
presence and role in our existence.

(Short Pause)

And the snow smiles.
Harmonic Earth conditions.

Just breathing... at your own pace... and picturing the Mother
Earth.
Loving... and appreciating her... and smiling with her.
Spending time with her.

And the cloud builds... and fills the sky... and you embrace
it... love it... respect it... and treasure its presence and role in
our existence.

(Short Pause)

And the cloud smiles.
Harmonic Earth conditions.

Just breathing… at your own pace… and picturing the Mother
Earth.
Loving… and appreciating her… and smiling with her.
Spending time with her.

And the rain pours down… soaking the earth's crust… and you
embrace it… love it… respect it… and treasure its presence
and role in our existence.

(Short Pause)

And the rain smiles.
Harmonic Earth conditions.

Just breathing… at your own pace… and picturing the Mother
Earth.
Loving… and appreciating her… and smiling with her.
Spending time with her.

And the sun shines through the clouds… warming and shining
down upon the earth's crust… and you embrace it… love it…
respect it… and treasure its presence and role in our existence.

(Short Pause)

And the sun smiles.
Harmonic Earth conditions.

Just breathing… at your own pace… and picturing the Mother
Earth.
Loving and appreciating her and smiling with her.
Spending time with her… and thanking her.

(Pause)

Now… that you have thanked the Mother Earth… you take a
deep breath.

PLANET HEALING FROM THE COSMOS

Gently breathing in... and out.
See yourself sitting together in a circle... glowing... with sparkling white energy.

Providing you with a safe and protected space.

(Pause)

Feel the companionship... and unity... between all those you sit with... in the circle.
Connected with love... for the planet.

(Pause)

Now see and feel... coloured light rays... enter the centre of the circle... and surround the group.
The light rays... are every colour of the rainbow.
Enjoy this spectacular sensation... of colour healing.

(Pause)

Knowing that you are safe... and protected.
You relax more... and more.
Gently breathing... at your own pace.
Gently breathing... in... and out.
Relaxing... and feeling calm.

Now that you are relaxed... the cosmos sends a range of spectacular phenomena... to delight you.

(Short Pause)

Into the centre of the circle... arrive five shooting stars... two sparkling comets... an asteroid... and three meteorites... and other spectacular phenomena.

(Short Pause)

Glorious white light surrounds all the spectacular phenomena.
Enjoy this amazing sight now.

(Pause)

These phenomena... are not only here to delight you... they
are here to act as your guide... and protector... throughout this
meditation.

(Short Pause)

You find yourself particularly drawn... to one of the
phenomena... that the cosmos has sent.
This is your guide for the meditation.
You go with your shooting star... comet... asteroid... or
meteorite... and know that you are safe... and protected.

(Short Pause)

You slowly ascend... into the atmosphere... watching the
Earth as it appears to get smaller... and smaller... the higher...
and higher... you go.
Feeling lighter... and lighter.
You feel so much lighter.

(Pause)

You leave your earthly worries behind you... as you go higher
and higher.
Feeling so much lighter.

(Pause)

Earth looks so small... from where you are.
Your attention is drawn... to the spectacular sights that are all
around you.
The sun.
The moon.
The many stars... and other planets.
You also notice planets... that have not yet been discovered.
The view is one of the most beautiful... that you have ever
seen.
Absorb it now.

(Pause)

You feel safe... and secure... with your shooting star...
comet... asteroid... or meteorite.
You turn and view the Earth.
Your particular guiding phenomenon... helps you send love to
the planet Earth.
You send love... to the planet Earth... in your own very
special way.
The whole group... sends love to the planet Earth...
simultaneously.
All connected... as the universe is one.

(Pause)

As you send love... to the planet Earth... the Earth glows
pink... and green.
Heaviness lifts... from the Earth... and the Earth becomes
trouble free.
See the Earth peaceful now.
The Earth is so peaceful now.

(Pause)

Your shooting star... comet... asteroid... or meteorite... now
takes you on an amazing journey.
A journey just for you... where great knowledge is given.
Spend time now... with your guiding phenomenon... and
enjoy your individual journey.
Travel now... with your particular guiding phenomenon... to
that special place.

(Long Pause)

Now that you have gained much... and seen much... it is time
for you to return.
Your shooting star... comet... asteroid... or meteorite...
guides you back.
Returning to Earth.

(Short Pause)

Guiding you back… through the universe.
Past the stars.
Past the sun.
Past the planets.
Past the moon.
Returning to Earth.

(Short Pause)

The Earth looks larger… as you get closer.
It shines that wonderful pink… and green glow… and it is a safe place to return to.

(Pause)

Retuning to Earth.
Coming back… back to Earth… back to your body… back to the circle… back to the seat that you are sitting in.

(Short Pause)

You say farewell to the guiding phenomena… as they one by one shoot back into the cosmos with spectacular light.
You notice you have a medallion around your neck… with the symbol of the phenomenon that you travelled with.
This has been left with you… as special gift… and reminder of this experience.

You breathe deeply.

HEALING WORLD CRISIS

Relaxing your body... as you breathe.
Relaxing your muscles... and feeling calm.
Aware of all the protective white light... that surrounds you.
Feel the protective white light growing in intensity... extending from your body.
You feel safe... and relaxed.
Aware that there are pure divine spiritual helpers in the room... to assist in this healing evening.

You feel very relaxed... and calm.
Just breathing... feeling peaceful.

Above your head... you notice a beautiful bright star.
It's shining so brightly.
You feel even calmer.
The light from this special star... flows through your body... it extends all around you.
Feel the light expanding... filling the room.

(Pause)

Feel the healing light, extend around the whole planet.

(Pause)

The planet shines with this pure, divine, healing light... from this special star.
Feel the tension fade away from planet Earth... healed by the light.

(Pause)

The planet looks so different now... more peaceful.
See... and feel the peace... and love now.
We all have special healing talents... send love and healing... in your own very special way to our planet now.

See... and feel the planet benefit from this healing.
Notice the peace that spreads across the planet.
See the planet as serene.

(Pause)

Send love... peace... and understanding... in your own very special way to those all around the world.
Send comfort... and hope... to those who have been in despair.
See people all around the world... free from pain and suffering.
See tension and worry lift from people's shoulders.
See understanding and compassion dissolve conflicts around the world.

Send healing in your own very special way to [insert name of country]... those living there... visiting... and those affected by the recent events.
Send healing now.

(Pause)

See [insert name of country] surrounded in healing light.

What colour is the light being sent?

(Pause)

See this healing being received... and accepted.

Send healing and love to all those injured in [insert name of country].
See the healing process accelerate.
See emotions and traumas heal miraculously.
Send healing to the injured.
Send healing to their families.
Send healing to their friends... and those working so hard to assist at this time.

(Pause)

Send healing and comfort into the hospitals.
Healing light enters the very source of each illness or injury.
See the healing process accelerate.

See all those that have been affected in some way...
surrounded in healing light and energy.
See those affected absorbing the healing light and energy now.
See those affected healed and happy now.

Send healing and love to those who have tragically lost
friends... and loved ones in [insert name of country].
Send love to help their grieving process.
Offer a flower with love... in remembrance to those whose
lives have been lost in [insert name of country].

See [insert name of country] healing... and the economy and
livelihood recovering.
See [insert name of country] surrounded in the love and light
that is.

See the world whole.
See it as a peaceful place... where everyone is respected...
where compassion and understanding for each other is valued.
See a relaxed and peaceful world... surrounded in the love and
light that is.

(Pause)

You take a deep breath... and you notice the star again...
shining over your head.
The star shines over the world... continuing to let light and
healing energy reach all those who need it.
The light from this star takes you home.

(Short Pause)

Aware of the wonderful role you played in the world healing...
you take a deep breath.

KINDNESS SHOWERED DOWN UPON YOU

Breathing deeply.

Becoming aware of how safe and protected you are... as you breathe in the love from the universe.
Nothing to fear... as you are always taken care of.
Safe and protected... always.

Breathing in... the love of the universe.
Aware of the sensations... this creates in your body.
Feeling your body tingle... and your heart centre cleansed... as you breathe in the love from the universe.
Becoming lighter... and brighter.

(Short Pause)

See your aura extend.
A bright white light surrounds you... as it extends.
You see an angelic being before you.
You feel this being's pure kindness... as you look into its eyes.
You communicate telepathically with this being... as you make heart felt eye contact.

(Pause)

Stars light up the sky... and kindness is showered down upon you.
Love fills your heart... with an understanding of all.

(Short Pause)

The angelic being before you… is one of the many guardians of the planet… and is here to help you experience love… and kindness… so that you can help others experience it too.

The angelic being extends both its hands… and fills your heart with the purest love.

(Short Pause)

Kindness shines from your eyes… and everyone that you meet is touched by this gentle loving presence… with which you shine.

(Short Pause)

Making someone's day… by your smile… and the shine in your eyes.

Pure kindness shines upon all those you meet… having a peaceful effect.
Love and kindness is so easily spread around the world.
And you play an important part… as you shine kindness upon all those that you meet.

(Short Pause)

You encounter many people in your life… and you become aware of how you help and show kindness.
You become aware… that you make people's day.

(Pause)

Perhaps with your smile.
The sparkle in your eyes… or kind words that have connected with their heart and soul.

(Pause)

Maybe you have listened to someone that needed to talk.
Given financial assistance… or provided essentials for life.

(Pause)

Shine your kindness on everybody you meet… and see the affect this has on your life and the planet.

(Short Pause)

The angelic being is so pleased with you... and wants you to be aware of how many people's hearts you touch.

Spend some time communicating with the angelic being... in whatever way you find easiest.
Spend some time communicating now.

(Long Pause)

You are now worry free... feeling peaceful and full of kindness. The angelic being reminds you that you are safe... and protected... and smiles at you... as kindness shines from your eyes and your smile.
You thank the angelic being... and take a deep breath... and become aware of your physical body.

BUTTERFLIES
IN THE PINE FOREST

Breathing deeply… as you walk into a pine forest.
Walking deep into a beautiful old pine forest.
Feeling the soft pine needles under your feet… as you walk deeper into the forest.

(Pause)

You sit in the middle of the forest… surrounded by tall pine trees.
Just resting… surrounded by trees.
The breeze blows gently… and sunlight filters through the trees.
Your body relaxes… and you smile… as the sun touches your skin.

(Pause)

Whilst in the pine forest… you rest your eyes… and as you do… the image of a butterfly appears in your mind's eye… connecting you with the truth of your soul.
Concentrate for a moment on this beautiful image of the butterfly.

(Pause)

You look around the pine forest… and see a group of beautiful butterflies.
The sunlight streams through the forest… and the colours of the butterflies' wings… glisten in the sun.

You slowly blink your eyes… and you find the butterflies begin spiralling around your body… filling your life with joy.

(Pause)

The wind whispers... and brings you a message on the wings of these beautiful creatures.

(Pause)

Feel your spirit soar... as the butterflies dance around your body.
Transforming your life with grace and ease.
Feel the joy... and the colour that these butterflies bring into your life.

(Pause)

Now see 1000 violet butterflies... ever so gently... circle around your body.
Feel the joy... and transformation... that the violet butterflies bring to into your life.

(Pause)

2 indigo butterflies... ever so gently circle around your body.
Feel the joy... and transformation... that the indigo butterflies bring into your life.

(Pause)

16 bright blue butterflies... ever so gently... circle around your body.
Feel the joy... and transformation... that the bright blue butterflies bring into your life.

(Pause)

12 green and pink butterflies... ever so gently... circle around your body.
Feel the joy... and transformation... that the green and pink butterflies bring into your life.

(Pause)

10 yellow butterflies... ever so gently... circle around your body.
Feel the joy... and transformation... that the yellow butterflies bring into your life.

(Pause)

6 orange butterflies... ever so gently... circle around your body.

Feel the joy... and transformation... that the orange butterflies bring into your life.

(Pause)

4 red butterflies... ever so gently... circle around your body.
Feel the joy... and transformation... that the red butterflies bring into your life.

(Pause)

Feeling full of joy... you now send the butterflies out into the world.
The butterflies flutter... and fly up into the sunlight... that filters through the tall pine trees.

(Pause)

The butterflies fly out into the world... healing and transforming any disharmony in the world.
Bringing joy... and sweetness... to the whole of mankind.
Send the butterflies out into the world with love.

(Pause)

Now bring your focus back to the pine forest.
You walk back through the pine forest... feeling the soft pine needles beneath your feet.

(Short Pause)

Feeling refreshed... and full of joy... you walk back through the pine forest...

Taking a moment to say thank you.

BECOME ONE
WITH THE TREES

In your mind's eye… you see a tree.
See a willow tree.

(Pause)

And let that image fade away.
See a wattle tree.

(Pause)

And let that image fade away.
See an apple tree.

(Pause)

And let that image fade away.
See a peppercorn tree.

(Pause)

And let that image fade away.
See an oak tree.

(Pause)

And let that image fade away.

The image of the trees flickers through your mind.
The willow tree… the wattle tree… the apple tree… the
peppercorn tree… the oak tree.

One stands out to you.
Maybe it is a different tree altogether.
Just focus on the tree that comes to mind.

(Pause)

Focus on that special tree… on its branches… on its leaves…
and on its trunk and root system.

Let the essence of the tree wash over you.
You become more and more relaxed... as you focus on the essence of the tree.

Just breathing... gently breathing.
Just relaxing with each breath... as you focus on the tree.
Focusing on the tree... letting the essence of the tree wash over you.
Washing over you ever so gently.

As you breathe... you become aware of your torso.
You become aware of the trunk of the tree.
Let your torso become the trunk of the tree... as the essence of the tree... ever so gently washes over you.

(Pause)

As you breathe... you become aware of the soles of your feet.
You become aware of the roots of the tree.
Let the soles of you feet become the roots of the tree... as the essence of the tree... ever so gently washes over you.

(Pause)

As you breathe... you become aware of your arms... shoulders... and head.
You become aware of the branches... and leaves of the tree.
Let your arms... shoulders... and head... become the branches and leaves of the tree... as the essence of the tree... ever so gently washes over you.

(Pause)

Be the tree.
See yourself as the tree.

(Pause)

Totally connected with its essence.
Be as one with the tree.

Breathing... one with the tree.
Breathing in the energy from the sky... through your leaves.

Breathing in the energy from the sky... through your leaves and branches... to your trunk.

(Pause)

Breathing in the energy from the sky... through your leaves and branches... down your trunk... to your root system.

(Pause)

Breathing in the energy from the sky... through your leaves and branches... down your trunk... down into your root system... and now down deep into the core of the Earth.

(Pause)

Breathing in the wonderful energy from the sky.

(Pause)

A beautiful rainbow appears in the sky... so many colours.
You breathe in the violet ray of the rainbow.
See your leaves turn violet... as you breathe in the violet ray... bringing the violet ray in through your leaves... through your trunk... through your root system... and down deep into the core of the Earth.
One with the tree... and one with the Earth.

(Pause)

You breathe in the indigo ray of the rainbow.
See your leaves turn indigo... as you breathe in the indigo ray...bringing the indigo ray in through your leaves... through your trunk... through your root system... and down deep into the core of the Earth.
One with the tree... and one with the Earth.

(Pause)

You breathe in the blue ray of the rainbow.
See your leaves turn blue... as you breathe in the blue ray...
bringing the blue ray in through your leaves... through your
trunk... through your root system... and down deep into the
core of the Earth.
One with the tree... and one with the Earth.

(Pause)

You breathe in the green ray of the rainbow.
See your leaves turn green... as you breath in the green ray...
bringing the green ray in through your leaves... through your
trunk... through your root system... and down deep into the
core of the Earth.
One with the tree... and one with the Earth.

(Pause)

You breathe in the yellow ray of the rainbow.
See your leaves turn yellow... as you breathe in the yellow
ray... bringing the yellow ray in through your leaves... through
your trunk... through your root system... and down deep into
the core of the Earth.
One with the tree... and one with the Earth.

(Pause)

You breathe in the orange ray of the rainbow.
See your leaves turn orange... as you breathe in the orange
ray... bringing the orange ray in through your leaves... through
your trunk... through your root system... and down deep into
the core of the Earth.
One with the tree... and one with the Earth.

(Pause)

You breathe in the red ray of the rainbow.
See your leaves turn red... as you breathe in the red ray...
bringing the red ray in through your leaves... through your
trunk... through your root system... and down deep into the
core of the Earth.
One with the tree... and one with the Earth.

Gaia... the Mother Earth... sends energy up through your root system... up through your trunk... through your branches and leaves... and out into the atmosphere.

(Short Pause)

Feel your connection with the Mother Earth.

(Long Pause)

Now that you have spent some time connecting with the essence of the tree... the energy of the sky... and your connection to the Earth...
You return to your physical body... taking a few moments to give thanks as you breathe deeply.

COLOURFUL HEALING FROGS

Just breathing... as you sit in a circle... with your eyes gently shut.
Feeling relaxed... and very peaceful.
Breathing the cool fresh air.
Feeling so tranquil.

(Pause)

You become aware... that in the centre of the circle... that you are sitting in... there is a beautiful... clear... sparkling pond.
So cool... so calm.
Breathing in the fresh air... you become more... and more relaxed... with each moment that goes by.

(Pause)

In this pond... there are so many frogs... sitting on lily pads.
Hear their gentle croaking... and splashing.
These frogs... are multi coloured.
Some have two colours.
Some have three colours.
See the colours of the rainbow... in these frogs.
They are healing frogs.

(Long Pause)

The pond is so clear.
Sparkles... and light shine brightly... from the pond... it is illuminated.
The sound of the water... is calming... and the frogs gentle croaking... relaxes you... with each passing moment.

(Pause)

Feeling calm... you become aware of your heart centre.
Your body begins to illuminate... with white light...just like the sparkling pond.

You ease your bare feet... into the water.
The water is cool... and very cleansing.
Your body is overcome with a tingling sensation... that begins
to wash away any tension... or fear... that has collected in your
body over time.

(Pause)

Washed away... are any worries about your life... or the world
in which you live.

(Short Pause)

Your heart centre begins to pulse.
Feel this sensation in the middle of your chest... as you move
your feet in the water.
A gentle warm glow... spreads throughout your body... and
you realise... that one of those coloured healing frogs is there
for you.
It is there to heal any pain... any fear... any sorrow... or
hesitation... you have about living your life to the best of your
ability.

(Pause)

This frog jumps into your heart centre now.
See it jump into you heart centre.
It is there for your healing.

(Pause)

Feel the healing take place... with the assistance of this loving
frog.
Feel the cleansing.
Feel the relief.

(Short Pause)

Now feeling happier... and lighter.
Feel your spirit dance with joy.
Love for yourself... and love for others.

(Pause)

Happy hearts and love for others... makes for a peaceful world.
Feel your spirit dance with joy... in this peaceful world.

(Pause)

Send a colourful healing frog... from the pond... to someone... somewhere else in the world.

(Short Pause)

Release these colourful healing frogs... into the world.
See people's hearts heal.
See people free from fear... free from sorrow... free from anger... feeling happy... and lighter.
See their spirit dance with joy.

(Pause)

See a happy peaceful world... that you have helped create.

With your heart centre now cleansed... and healed... you feel happy... and you splash your feet in the pond.

(Pause)

The healing frog... jumps from your heart centre... back into the pond... and onto a lily pad... and then onto the next lily pad.
Helping you take the next step in your life.

(Pause)

You thank this little frog... for the healing... and you know that you may return to this special pond... any time you feel the need for healing.

You feel light... and alive.
Ready to go out into the world... and be.
Ready to go forward.
You breathe deeply.

SUNFLOWERS

Concentrating on your breath.
You sit in a green, grassy meadow relaxing in nature.
The sun shines… and it is warm.
Beautiful golden-coloured rays from the sun… shine down on you.

Golden-coloured rays… flowing down through your crown chakra…filling your body… full of golden coloured rays.

The golden-coloured rays continue to flow down through your brow chakra.
Golden-coloured rays… flowing down to your throat chakra.
Golden-coloured rays… flowing down to your heart chakra.
Golden-coloured rays… flowing down to your solar plexus chakra.
Golden-coloured rays… flowing down to your sacral chakra.
Golden-coloured rays… flowing down to your base chakra.
Golden-coloured rays… filling your whole body.

(Pause)

The sun's golden-coloured rays… flow through your body… and into the Earth's core.
Such beautiful rays.

You sit peacefully in the green, grassy meadow… with a beautiful sunflower on your lap.
This sunflower brings you many golden-coloured rays.
Encouraging you to be radiant and full of joy.

You stare into the face of the sunflower… that rests in your lap.
A golden-coloured glow surrounds your body… and any childhood pains are lifted.
The sunflower transports you back to your perfect child-like essence.

Light... free... innocent... fun loving... full of energy and intrigue.

(Short Pause)

You play in the green, grassy meadow... fascinated by the many sunflowers that now surround you.

(Long Pause)

You may share this sunflower healing with others in the world.

(Pause)

Still connected to your perfect child-like essences... you share the power of the sunflower with the children in [insert name of country].
You give the children in [insert name of country] some of the sunflower seeds... from the centre of the sunflower.
The children plant the seeds... and the sunflowers grow... bringing the children many golden-coloured rays.
Encouraging them to shine radiant and full of joy... healing any of their childhood pains.

(Pause)

The children of [insert name of country] share the seeds from the sunflowers with their family... and the sunflowers spread throughout the land... bringing golden-coloured rays to the people throughout [insert name of country].

(Pause)

You now come back to the green, grassy meadow... and spend some time just for you.

(Pause)

Spend some time with the sunflowers in the field... healing and connecting with your pure... radiant... essence.

(Long Pause)

Radiant and glowing... you say thank you.

THE DOVES OF PURE PEACE

As you relax… you see a white dove fly towards you.
The dove brings a message of peace and harmony to your life.
You feel so calm… as the dove lands near you.
Your body feels so much lighter.
You see beautiful colours… all around you… and around the
dove is a golden-coloured glow.

You feel peace… like you have never felt before.
This feeling extends… and grows.
See this feeling of pure peace… glowing brighter and brighter.
This peace… extends to your friends and loved ones.
See them calm… and peaceful.
You now feel lighter… and brighter… and even more peaceful.

The pure peace intensifies.

You see two more doves arrive… they land nearby.
The doves have increased the peaceful energy.

(Short Pause)

Let your body heal… with the sensations of pure peace.
This peaceful energy extends… throughout the town you live
in.

(Short Pause)

The whole town glows… with this pure peace… making it a
beautiful place in which to live.
The pure peace intensifies.

More white doves arrive.
They are attracted to the peaceful energy.
As the doves arrive the pure peace increases… and in turn
attract more white doves.
The peacefulness increases… and you relax deeper and deeper.

This pure peace is so powerful.
It heals all hurts.
Feel any old wounds heal... as you are surrounded by the love
of pure peace.

You see this pure peace extend... further... and further.
See the pure peace extend... all around the country.

(Short Pause)

The pure peace heals all those with whom it comes into
contact.
The whole country glows with this pure peace.
And more doves arrive.

This pure peace is so powerful.
The pure peace extends over the oceans... healing and
cleansing the water... and all that live in it.

(Short Pause)

The doves spread... and fly over the ocean.
This pure peace is so powerful and strong... that it attracts
other doves.
You are so relaxed in this pure peace.
The pure peace... has built up to a level that has beneficial
effects on the whole world.
See the pure peace extend.

(Short Pause)

See the pure peace extend all around the world.

(Short Pause)

See the pure peace healing all those it comes in contact with.

(Short Pause)

The world now glows… with this pure and peaceful energy…
and the doves appear everywhere.
See people all around the world… from all different cultures…
feeling peaceful… and calm.
See them surrounded by the doves… of pure peace.

Our world… greatly benefits… from the energy of pure peace.

(Short Pause)

Take some time to bathe in the pure peace… and relax.

(Pause)

You are now rejuvenated and very relaxed.
Feeling so calm… and peaceful.
Your dove is still beside you.
It never left your side.

(Short Pause)

Your dove slowly brings you back to your physical body… you
say thank you and farewell for now… and breathe deeply.

THE SOIL AND THE SUN SHOWER

You take a deep breath and you find yourself walking on a piece of land... a special part of the Earth.

(Short Pause)

Notice the country you are in.
Notice the land and the soil you are walking on.
Notice the colours... of the soil.
Notice the texture... and the feel of the land and the soil.
Notice the scenery all around you.

(Pause)

Rest there on the land.
Sitting on the ground... feeling the land and soil with your hands.

Appreciating nature.

Appreciating the land... and the soil.

(Short Pause)

Rest there on the land.

Thanking the land... and the soil... for the crops it has grown... and the nutrients it has supplied.

Thanking the land... and the soil... for supporting the trees and plant life.

Thanking the land... and the soil... for providing shelter for the animals that burrow in the ground.

Thanking the land... and the soil... for the abundance of fossil fuels.

Thanking the land... and the soil... for the healing crystals that are available to us.

(Short Pause)

Appreciating... and thanking the land... and the soil... for all that it provides.

(Pause)

Gentle rain begins to sprinkle... as you rest there on the land.

A beautiful sun shower.

(Short Pause)

The rain is pleasant and comfortable on your skin.
It is gentle and refreshing.
Revitalising you... and the land.

(Long Pause)

Such a beautiful sun shower.

The rain smells so fresh... and clean.

(Pause)

Such a beautiful sun shower.
You feel revitalised... as the rain gently and pleasantly...
touches your skin.
You breathe in the smell of the rain... as it gently sprinkles down.
The land absorbs what it needs... and replenishes.

(Pause)

Ever so gently... the rain revitalises and replenishes the land.

(Long Pause)

A rainbow appears in the sky.
A reminder of the healing... that has just taken place.
The sun peeks through the clouds... high up in the sky... and the clouds clear.
The sun shines down... warming and revitalising your body.

(Pause)

You thank Mother Earth… and she thanks you.
You breathe deeply… and walk back across the revitalised land.
Walking back across the revitalised land.

LAND CARE IN AUSTRALIA

Breathing.

Your body regenerates... with each breath that you take.
Tensions fade away... as you relax.
Breathing.
Relaxing.
Resting in a field.

(Short Pause)

Grass as far as you can see.
A field that was cleared many years ago.
You breathe in... and feel the energy of this old land that you
are resting on.

(Short Pause)

Just breathing... as your body regenerates with each breath.

Resting... aware of the natural potential of the earth.

(Short Pause)

You notice a single bird fly overhead.
It drops a seed... a seed full of potential.

The sun shines... and the seed begins to germinate.

(Pause)

The seed breaks through the soil... and grows towards the sky.
A beautiful gum tree develops.

(Short Pause)

The tree grows stronger... as Mother Nature provides rain.

The sun shines... and the leaves multiply.

The warmth of the sun's rays intensify... and the gumnut pods drop... and shed their seeds into the warm earth... where they begin to germinate.

(Pause)

A kangaroo hops by... carrying seeds in its fur.
The kangaroo scratches... and the seeds drop.

(Short Pause)

Mother Nature provides rain.

The sun shines... and the seeds germinate... growing into wattle trees.

(Pause)

Birds arrive to live in the trees.

The wind blows... carrying seeds from the trees to other parts of the field that you're resting on.

These seeds also begin to germinate.

(Pause)

Koalas return to the gum trees.
Bees unite with the wattle... pollinating the flowers and making honey.

(Short Pause)

As the land regenerates... you feel relaxed.
You breathe deeply.
Your body regenerates... with each breath that you take.

Relaxing... as the bees pollinate the native flowers.

(Short Pause)

Relaxing... as the birds drink the nectar from the flowers... and spread the seeds.

(Short Pause)

Relaxing... as the animals return.

(Long Pause)

The wind blows... and the seeds from the plants spread.
The foliage grows... and animals feed.

The field is rebalanced... as it regenerates.
A peaceful place has been created for you.

(Short Pause)

Feel the energy of this regenerated land.

Feel your body... regenerated... full of energy... back in balance.
Feel the sun on you skin... the wind in your hair... the earth under your feet.

Smell the fragrances of the native plants.

(Short Pause)

A small native bird lands on your shoulder... chirping cheerfully... thanking you for your assistance in this regeneration process.

Relaxed... re-energised by nature... and amazed by the potential of the earth... you thank Mother Nature.
In touch with the beautiful fragrances of the bush... you take a deep breath... and become aware of your physical body.

FERN

Taking a deep breath.
Resting cross-legged... on the ground... eyes closed.
Cocooned... encased... by the colour green.
Long... lush... green leaves... wrap around your body.
Cocooned... encased... by the colour green.
Part of the ground... the earth... the tropical rainforest.

(Short Pause)

Cocooned... encased... by the colour green.
Moist... fresh water droplets... nourish you.
Cool... clean air... refreshes... and provides nourishment and nutrients.

(Short Pause)

The sounds of birds... penetrate through the cocooned... encased... long green leaves... that gently wrap around your body.
Surrounded by the sounds of birds... tranquil.

(Short Pause)

Light shines through the cocooned, encasing leaves... and you are connected to the earth.
Gentle... soft, nurturing light... filters down.
Connected... cross-legged... on the ground.
Drawing strength through the nutrients of the earth.

(Short Pause)

Stretching towards the soft... and gentle light.
One by one... ever so slowly... the long... lush... green leaves... unfold from your body.
Growth.
Expansion.
Opening... to those gentle rays of light.

Opening... and surrendering... to the purity of the universe.

(Pause)

Reaching tall... into the beautiful tropical rainforest.
You are surrounded by ferns.
You are connected with the ferns.
You are One.

(Pause)

Open to the universe.
All... is in balance.
All... is provided for.
All needs... are met.

(Short Pause)

You sit and admire... this tropical rainforest... that you are a part of.

(Short Pause)

Glistening rays of light... filter through the tree foliage.
The trees are so tall... and so wide.
Vines climb the trunks of the trees.
Moss grows... at the base of the trees... near the root systems.
Insects live in the moist fallen leaves.
Dew rests in droplet form... on the ferns that are unfolding.
Sounds of the birds echo... throughout the forest.

(Short Pause)

So clean... and so fresh.
So invigorating... and oh, so easy to breathe.

You are open to the power of our pure universe.
Your aura is cleansed... and emanates the colour green.

(Short Pause)

You contemplate what this colour means for you at this time...
and its connection with the tropical rainforest... that you are so
much a part of.

(Short Pause)

Slowly you walk through the rainforest... and admire. Walking through the rainforest and breathing deeply.

(Pause)

Taking a deep breath... you become aware of your physical body.

AROMAS OF THE GARDEN

Breathing deeply.
You concentrate on your breath… as you walk through a beautiful garden.
The garden is full of many healing plants.

There are so many varieties of healing plants in this beautiful garden… and the aromas from the plants are sensational.

(Pause)

You breathe in the aromas… as you walk through this beautiful healing garden.

(Short Pause)

As you breathe in the beautiful aromas… your body relaxes.
Feel the deep relaxation in your body.
Feel any tension drift away.
Feeling totally relaxed now… as you walk through the garden.

(Pause)

As you walk through the beautiful healing garden… you come across the sweet fennel plant.
It has fine feathery green leaves… and a flower on a long green stem.

The liquorice fragrance permeates your whole body as you run your hands through the fine green leaves of the plant.
You find that your stomach and digestive system relax and settle.

(Short Pause)

You continue to walk through the beautiful healing garden.
The liquorice aroma of the sweet fennel plant fades… and you notice a well established tree with gum resin oozing from its trunk.

The myrrh fragrance permeates your whole body... as you touch the gum resin from the tree.
You find that you become still... and centred... and your breathing eases.

(Short Pause)

You continue to walk through the beautiful healing garden. The myrrh aroma of the gum resin... from the tree fades... and you find a jasmine vine... with many small flowers.

The jasmine fragrance permeates your whole body... as you breath in the sweet perfume of the flowers.
You find that you become conscious of the "now" moment... as your life is filled with passion.

(Short Pause)

Soothed and relaxed... you continue to walk through the beautiful healing garden.
The jasmine aroma fades... and you discover a large lavender plant.

The lavender fragrance permeates your whole body... as you run your hands through the mass of purple flowers.
You experience a deeper state of relaxation... and you feel protected.
Your skin is soothed... and any tension is relieved.

(Short Pause)

You continue to walk through the beautiful healing garden. The lavender aroma fades... and you see a patch of camomile growing wild... with white flowers and many petals.

The camomile fragrance permeates your whole body... and you have permission to make a necklace with the flowers.
You find that your body begins to let go... removing limitations from life.

(Short Pause)

You continue to walk through the beautiful healing garden…
and you discover a bubbling natural spring.

The water is warm and inviting… and a special healing plant
grows all around the edge of the spring.
This healing plant is just right for your body.
The healing properties of the plant fill the natural spring… as
you bathe in the warm water.

Bathing… Healing… Absorbing whatever your body needs.

(Short Pause)

Rest there in the warm water for as long as you need to.

(Long Pause)

Resting… Healing… Absorbing all that your body needs.

(Short Pause)

You now walk back through the beautiful healing garden.
Walking back through the beautiful healing garden.

(Short Pause)

Relaxed and rejuvenated, you breathe deeply.

SHARE GIFTS OF LOVE

Standing safely on the top of a cliff... watching the ocean... as it stretches out all the way to the horizon.
The water glistens... as the sun shines down.
Your arms are stretched out either side of you... and you tilt your head up to the sun... to take its beautiful, beaming rays... deep into your body.

Breathing deeply... on this glorious day.
Taking in the beautiful rays from the sun.
Feel the breeze gently... and softly... brush past your skin.
As you stand on the cliff-top... with your arms stretched out... sun beaming down on you... warming and revitalising your body.

Take in as much as you can.
Taking in this very precious moment.

(Short Pause)

Over your shoulder is a bag.
It is light... but full of many special gifts.
These endless... unlimited gifts... enable you to heal... and express love to anyone... anything... anywhere in the world.
Reach into your bag... and explore the abundances of gifts of love.

(Short Pause)

Maybe...
Your bag contains food for the hungry.
Maybe...
Your bag contains special healing crystals.
Maybe...
Your bag contains seeds to replenish the forests.
Maybe...
Your bag contains magical fairy dust.

Maybe…
Your bag contains healing herbs and elixirs.
Maybe…
Your bag contains the most amazing healing energy.
Maybe…
Your bag contains hope for those in need.
Maybe…
Your bag contains moonbeams.
Maybe…
Your bag contains rainbows… that bring the rain for our Earth.

Your bag is full of endless gifts of love… for you to use in loving ways.
With this in mind… you push off on your toes and fly.
You fly through the air with ease… flying to share your gifts of love.
Enjoying the experience… you fly through the clouds.

Reaching into your bag… to share gifts of love with the atmosphere.
Giving our atmosphere whatever is needed.

(Pause)

Enjoying the experience you fly to [insert name of country].

(Short Pause)

Reaching into your bag to share gifts of love with [insert name of country].
Giving [insert name of country] whatever is needed.

(Short Pause)

Knowing you are safe… you fly down and mingle with the people in [insert name of country].
You reach into your bag… and share gifts of love…with the people in [insert name of country].

(Short Pause)

You push off on your toes… and fly.

(Short Pause)

Enjoying the experience... you fly to [insert name of another country].

(Short Pause)

Reaching into your bag... to share gifts of love with [insert name of country].
Giving [insert name of country] whatever is needed.

(Short Pause)

Knowing you are safe... you fly down and mingle with the people of [insert name of country].
You reach into your bag... and share gifts of love with the people of [insert name of country].

(Short Pause)

You push off on your toes... and fly.
You fly back to the cliff-top... and rest.
Resting on this glorious day.
Just taking in the rays of the sun... as you rest on the cliff-top.
Gently revitalising your body.

(Pause)

Now that you are rested... and rejuvenated... you take a deep breath.

LADY OF THE LAKE

Concentrating on your breathing... as you gently breathe in...
and out... at your own pace.
Breathing... and re-centring yourself.
Calm.

(Pause)

Surrounded by nature... you breath in... and out... at your
own pace.
You become one with the land... the lake... the trees and the
Earth... as you gently breathe in... and... out.
Calm.

(Pause)

And as you become centred... and one with the land... you
notice all the sounds of nature.
You notice the water rippling... across a beautiful lake.

(Pause)

You notice the sounds of the insects... and the chirping of the
birds.
And the grass sways in the breeze.

(Pause)

A beautiful parrot flies past... and yet there is a stillness... and
silence to the land.
Calm.

(Pause)

And as you breathe in... and out... the Earth washes away all
tension... that has been held in your body... and you feel
calm... perfectly calm.

(Pause)

And as you become aware of the calmness... you connect deeply with the Earth... nature and the beautiful lake.

(Short Pause)

A wave of deep appreciation of oneness... and the interconnectedness of life... washes over you... perfectly calm and one with the Earth.

(Pause)

All is well... and you are safe.
Protected in the arms of the Earth.
Calm.

(Pause)

As your sense of calmness deepens... the calmness... stillness... and the silence of the Earth... also deepens.

(Pause)

Calm.
One with nature and one with the lake.

(Pause)

And you and the Earth become one... and you move... and grow... at the most perfect pace.
Calm... and still... in this very moment.
Peaceful... and calm.

As your calmness deepens... so does the Earth's.
Peaceful... calm... and still.

(Short Pause)

The birds sing... in the background of the stillness... and silence of the land.
And the sounds of the water... of the beautiful lake... soften... to perfect stillness.

(Pause)

And you continue to breathe in... and out.
Experiencing the calmness of the Earth.

(Pause)

You see a reflection in the water.
As you look into the lake... you see the beautiful spirit... of
The Lady of the Lake... glimmer... and shine... on the surface
of the water.
And know that she is a reflection of your beauty... and she is
one with you... as you are one with the Earth.
Calm.

(Pause)

You have realised the interconnectedness of life... and have
experienced a deeper understanding and respect for the Earth.

(Short Pause)

And as you experience the deep sense of calm... so have
others.
Healing the Earth... and all that inhabit it.

A deep sense of calm... blesses you... the land... and the
Earth... as you breathe deeply.

DELIVERING PEACE

Breathing in the divine light.
Let it fill your whole body.
Feel the peace... and truth.
Feel the safety in this white light.
You shine brightly in this white light.
Peaceful.
Full of wisdom... and truth.

The divine light intensifies... and expands.
It's all around you.
You notice many white doves... encircling you in this bright light... that is surrounding you... and within you.

(Pause)

You picture the world... and as you do... Earth is surrounded... and protected in divine white light.
The light around the world intensifies in brightness... as you begin to focus.

Focusing on peace... as one of the many doves beside you... begins to fly.
You focus on [insert name of country]... and the dove arrives at [insert name of country] delivering peace.
Focusing on peace... and the bright divine light that is now surrounding [insert name of country].

[repeat the bold section many times, each time inserting the name of a different country]

Focusing on peace... as the remainder of the doves beside you... fly.
You focus on the world... the whole world... as the doves fly... delivering peace.
Focusing on peace... and the bright divine light... that is now surrounding the whole world.

So bright… the brightest light… surrounding the whole world.

You bring your attention back to your body.
You are surrounded in beautiful divine white light… and you
see the image of the dove that resides in your heart.

You smile… and breathe deeply.

OCEAN MERMAID

You concentrate on your breath… and breathe in the divine light… as you picture the ocean.
It is beautiful and still.
The sun shines down… and glistens on the surface of the water.
You smell the freshness of the saltwater.
The saltwater smell fills your body… and washes away any toxins.

(Pause)

The water is warm and inviting.
You bathe in the ocean.

Just floating in the saltwater… that is so fresh and still.
Just floating.
Feeling weightless.

So relaxing.

(Pause)

The water is so smooth against your skin.
Feeling weightless and buoyant… as you float in the water.
Your whole body… floating effortlessly in the ocean.

(Pause)

You feel your body transform… this happens easily… as you take the form of a fish.
You swim through the water with ease.
The water bubbles as you move your fins.

Gliding effortlessly through the water… you see the ocean in a totally new way.
All your worries are washed away by the saltwater… as you swim effortlessly through the ocean.

The sun filters through the water... and you see many colourful fish swim by.
You follow the colourful fish to a shimmering figure.

(Pause)

The figure is surrounded in light.
As you get closer... you see the figure is a kind-hearted mermaid.

You gently swim up to the mermaid.
She opens her hands... and you swim into her embrace.

(Short Pause)

You realise she is one of the guardians of the oceans... and that you are protected... and safe in her arms.
You feel your body transforming again...
In human form now... you are breathing easily in the water.
You speak and exchange words with the mermaid.

(Short Pause)

You feel so serene... as you join hands with the mermaid.
The beautiful caretaker of the ocean.
You communicate at length... about the importance of the oceans on our planet.

(Long Pause)

You communicate at length... about how you can help preserve the ocean... and the animals that live within it.

(Long Pause)

With this new knowledge... the mermaid takes you to the surface of the water.
You say farewell... to the guardian of the ocean.
You float weightlessly on the surface of the water... near the shore with the sun shining down on your skin.

(Short Pause)

You smile with the joy of your wonderful experience... and your new love for the ocean.

An understanding of the importance of the ocean... and all who live within it has been experienced.

You float weightlessly... and buoyantly... with the sun shining down.

Smiling... with your new love for the ocean.

As you smile... your new love for the ocean shines brightly through your aura... and extends out into the ocean.

This love and light... helps heal the ocean.

(Short Pause)

You float there near the shore... sending out your new love for the ocean.

(Long Pause)

You step out of the water onto the shore... sand beneath your feet.

(Short Pause)

Standing on the shore... sand beneath your feet.

The sun warms your body... and you breathe deeply.

THE TRUTH AND BEAUTY OF THE LAND

Breathe in… the divine light.
Let it fill your body.
Let it fill your whole body.

(Pause)

Breathe in… the divine light.
Feel it circulate throughout your body.

Feel the divine light… circulate and flow around your whole body.

(Pause)

See the divine light expand outward… through your aura.

(Pause)

Rest in the protecting light.
Peaceful… and calm.
Ready for an adventure of the mind.

As you breathe in… and out… connected with the divine light…you find yourself sitting in front of two trees… that are a little way apart from each other.

Just looking at the two trees.
A portal… or gateway… to the truth and beauty of the love that is our land… which we call Earth.

Notice where you are sitting… on this land we call Earth.
In your hometown?
Or maybe you are in another city… or even another country.
Just notice where you are.

(Pause)

Looking at the two trees... you see two guides.
Know that you are protected and safe.

One guide stays at the foot of the trees... and guards the gateway.
The other travels with you as a companion.

You walk with your guide companion... through the two trees... through the gateway... and find yourself in the truth and beauty of the love that is our land.

(Long Pause)

Clean air... bountiful water... clear skies.
Flourishing forms of nature.
Healthy, rich land... successful townships and enterprises.
Loving communication... harmony.
The truth and beauty of the love that is our land.

(Pause)

You wander with your guide companion.
Absorb and learn... in this truth and beauty of love that is our land.

(Long Pause)

Whilst wandering in the truth of this land...you are imparted with some knowledge... or understanding.
Receive the gift.

(Long Pause)

This knowledge or understanding... is for you to bring back into what is known as "the Now".
Knowledge or understanding... that needs reuniting with the Now of the land we call Earth.

You talk with your guides... and those who imparted the knowledge or understanding... and thank them for this gift bestowed.

(Pause)

You bow your head… acknowledging the understanding and knowledge imparted.
You turn and walk with your guide.
Walking…
Returning in the direction from which you came.
Walking…
Returning with your guide to the two trees… the portal or gateway.
Stepping through the two trees… back to the Now of the land from which you came.

Standing in front of the two trees… with both of your guides. They smile… and nod… as you take some time to impart the knowledge and understanding to those in the land of the Now.
See the knowledge and understanding well received.
See the knowledge and understanding re-united with the land.

(Pause)

Know that you have done well.
The two guides place their hands on your shoulders… and you feel a beautiful flutter of light surround and bless you… as you take a deep breath.

ROLLING RAIN CLOUDS

You breathe deeply... as a cloud appears in front of you.
You find yourself sitting... and relaxing on this cloud as it
drifts up into the sky.
Surrounded by universal energy... at one with all.
You sit and relax... on this cloud... and think about the rain...
rain for the Earth's highest good.

(Pause)

As you sit up on this rain bringing cloud... you see the sky
change... and the clouds move.
Rolling rain clouds move in... with the assistance of your
thoughts... and the nature spirits... we call upon.

(Pause)

And as you think about the Earth receiving the beautiful rain...
rain for Earth's highest good... the clouds respond.
The clouds spread... and move to the areas that need rain
most.

(Short pause)

Rolling rain clouds move in... with the assistance of your
loving thoughts and the nature spirits.
You continue to float... embraced by the magical rain cloud.
A gift from the [insert belief system i.e Creator/Great Spirit/
God/Goddess/Lord Buddha/all that is good, etc.]

And it begins to rain.
Beautiful rain.
Raining... replenishing the Earth.
Glorious rain... replenishing the Earth.
Filling the catchment areas.

Gently raining.
The rivers flow.
The dams are full.
The lakes glisten and shine as it rains.

(Pause)

And the land receives the rain that it needs.
Delicate rain.
Such beautiful rain.

(Pause)

As you breathe... and relax your body... the magical rain cloud that has you embraced... returns you to where you began... and you breathe deeply.

(Long Pause)

A rainbow appears... high up in the sky... and the clouds slowly, one by one fade away.

You see the clouds gently fade away... and you thank the nature spirits... and the [insert belief system i.e Creator/Great Spirit/God/Goddess/Lord Buddha/all that is good, etc.] for the rain.

WISDOM OF THE TREES

Breathing deeply... you walk peacefully through an ancient forest.
Walking peacefully... through the ancient forest.

(Short Pause)

You have a strong sense of connection... to the ancient Earth.
You feel at peace... as you walk among the trees in the forest.

Such ancient land... for which you have so much respect.
Respect for this land... with which you feel a strong sense of connection.

(Pause)

The trees are so old... so tall... so strong... and wise.
As you run your hand up the bark... of one of the wise ancient trees in this forest... you become aware of the importance of these trees to the Earth and mankind.

You feel so connected to the Earth... and have much respect for the trees.
You sit at the foot of one of these wise, ancient trees.
You place both your hands on the bark of one of these trees... and you relax.

You lean forward... and gently rest your forehead on the tree.
You have such a strong connection to these trees... and to the ancient forest.

You rest here... relax... and communicate with this wise, ancient tree.

(Short Pause)

Communicate with the tree... about the importance of the trees to the Earth.

(Pause)

Communicate with the tree... about the environment.

(Pause)

Communicate with the tree... about the air... and atmosphere.

(Pause)

Communicate with the tree... about the healing of Mother Earth.

(Pause)

Exchanging love and respect... as mankind and the trees share the Earth.

You now walk back through the ancient forest... with so much respect.

(Pause)

Walking back through the ancient forest... feeling grounded... and connected to the Earth...

You thank the ancient forest as you breathe deeply.

ANIMAL HEALING

Breathing in the refreshing air... as you peacefully... and quietly... sit on the top of a mountain.
Concentrating on your breath... while you peacefully sit on the top of a mountain.
As you breathe in... surrounded in protective light... you notice many healers surrounding you.

(Pause)

These healers are wearing headdresses... that symbolise in some way... the animals that they care for.

(Short Pause)

You breathe in... and one of the healers steps forward. You look at the headdress... and realise this healer cares for the [insert name of animal(s)]. The healer looks at you. You communicate telepathically.

(Pause)

You bow your head in respect... and acknowledgment... and send the healer out to all the [insert name of animal(s)] in the name of healing.

[repeat the bold section many times, inserting the name of a different animal each time]

You breathe in... and the healers return to you.
Surrounding you... as you sit on the top of the mountain.
In unison... the animal healers bow their heads to you... with respect and acknowledgement... and vanish.
You know that you can connect again... when the time is right.

(Short Pause)

You feel refreshed... and pleased with the healing that has just taken place.

BREATHE WITH THE TREE

You take a deep breath... and relax...
In front of you is a gate.
There is a wise person... angel... or animal guide... waiting
there for you... to guide and protect you.
You open the gate... and walk along the lush... green...grassy
pathway... escorted by your wise person... angel... or animal
guide.

You are guided to a large tree... a special tree.
Its trunk is so wide... its leaves are so green... and it sparkles
with energy.

(Short Pause)

It is such a peaceful place.
The air is so clear... so fresh... so easy to breathe.
Your aura strengthens... as you breathe in this clear... fresh
air.

(Short Pause)

You see your aura become clearer... and stronger.
See it extend... and expand... as you breathe.

(Short Pause)

You breathe... you breathe with the tree.
Becoming one... with the tree... as you breathe.

(Short Pause)

You breathe in the clean sparkling oxygen... from the air...
and breathe out carbon dioxide.
The tree breathes in carbon dioxide and exhales sparkling
oxygen.

(Short Pause)

You breathe in the sparkling oxygen from the air… becoming one with the tree.
And as you breathe out… the tree breathes in.
And as the tree breathes out… you breathe in.
Becoming one with the tree… as you breathe.

(Short Pause)

You breathe in the sparkling oxygen from the air… becoming one with the tree.
And as you breathe out… the tree breathes in.
And as the tree breathes out… you breathe in.
Becoming one with the tree… as you breathe.

Spend some time becoming one with the tree… breathing with the tree… sustaining each other.

(Long Pause)

The air sparkles with energy… and your aura is clear and strong… making you feel so healthy… with each breath that you take.
Breathing in the air that supports all of mankind.
Totally supported as you breathe.
You breathe with the tree… and the tree breathes with you.
One with each other.
One with Nature.
One with the Earth.

(Short Pause)

You are so relaxed.
You begin to communicate with the tree… and with Nature… as you are one with each other.

(Long Pause)

The tree is very old… and very wise.
Your connection is strong… as you breathe with each other.
You continue to communicate… as you are one with each other… and one with the Earth.

(Short Pause)

Breathing together... learning about the Earth... learning how to support each other.
Healing each other... as you breathe together.
Strengthening your aura with each breath.
You feel so healthy... with each breath that you take.

As you breathe in... the tree breathes out.
And as you breathe out... the tree breathes in.
There is a deep connection and love for each other.
A love for the interaction between Nature and humans.

Knowing that this connection is strong and everlasting... you thank the tree for this experience of oneness.

(Pause)

Now that you have thanked the tree...your wise person... angel... or animal guide... guides you back... along the lush, green, grassy pathway... and back through the gate.

(Short Pause)

You thank your wise person... angel... or animal guide and say farewell as you walk back through the gate.

CARETAKERS AND THE RING
OF TREES

As you breathe… you notice a beautiful garden before you.
You walk through the garden… to a circle of trees.
The air is cool and revitalising.
You approach the trees… that are growing in a perfect circle.
You become aware of the healing energy… that surrounds this
circle of trees… and is actually a part of them.
This is a very special and sacred place.

The leaves of the trees move slightly in the air.
Everything in this special place is in harmony.
You feel the peace… and connect with it.
All your worries fade… as you feel the peace in this very
special place.

(Pause)

You walk up to one of the trees… and sit down with your back
to the tree.
The trees' root systems runs deep into the earth… and you feel
the trees grounding you… and strengthen your connection to
the earth.

Your body is now rejuvenated… and you have a new sense of
wellbeing.
You feel relaxed… and peaceful… as you connect with the
tree.

(Pause)

All the trees are connected in that perfect circular
configuration.
You notice a person sitting at the foot of the other trees… one
person at each tree.
Everybody is relaxed… and has found a sense of wellbeing.

(Pause)

You recognise those sitting at the foot of the other trees from the meditation group... and some are dear friends that could not physically be here today.

Each at the foot of another tree... in there own safe... and sacred space.

Everyone is so relaxed... and peaceful.

The leaves of the trees occasionally rustle in the air... and you feel revitalized.

Absorbing the healing energy from this sacred place.

(Pause)

In the centre of the circle of the trees... you notice a group... of kind-hearted caretakers.

These caretakers... are caring for the plants and seedlings... that are growing in the centre of the circle of trees.

These plants and seedlings represent growth.

Growth of your goals... and aims in life.

The growth and development of the world.

(Short Pause)

You see what a supportive influence each of these caretakers has upon the Earth... and upon us.

You smile at the caretakers... and begin helping them.

Assisting in caring for the growth of mankind.

Tending.

Watering.

Nurturing your goals and aims in life.

Caring for the Earth... and plant life.

Growth blossoms.

(Pause)

With the inner realisation that there are always kind-hearted caretakers to assist us at every instance... in any way that is needed... you relax in the truth of a peaceful world... and return to the tree.

You sit beside the tree... and breathe deeply.
Thanking it.

(Pause)

The circle of trees fades.
You breathe a little deeper... and focus on the physical aspects of yourself... your physical body.

TRUE CONNECTION WITH SOUL

Focusing on your breath.
Breathing... seeing your soul shine.
Breathing... seeing your soul shine brighter... and brighter.
Any earthly worries lift... as you focus on your breath... and the light.
Your soul shines brighter... and brighter.

You are feeling so light... and bright... in touch with your true essence... so pure.
You shine so brightly... and you feel the true connection with your soul.

(Pause)

Your higher self radiates... and you feel connected with the universe.
You see the true essence of others... past their exterior.
You see the light that shines from all living beings... and you connect with their soul... the oneness of all.
You see their true essence.

(Pause)

You see others shine.
Their higher self radiates... see them connected with the universe.
In touch with their true essence... so pure... feeling the true connection with their soul.

One with all.

(Pause)

Now that you feel... the true connection with your soul... you picture a special place in nature.
You feel so connected to this special place.
You see and feel... the earth beneath you.
You smell the freshness... of the plant life.
You feel the breeze... brush past you skin... stimulating your senses.

(Pause)

At peace.
Connected to the Earth.
So in touch with Nature.

Gracefully... and so quietly... a group of butterflies... floats by on the breeze.

(Short Pause)

You are resting deeply now... so deeply.
Feeling peaceful... experiencing the true connection with your soul.

Resting so deeply now... no worries... they have all lifted... as you are in touch with your true nature.
The true connection with your soul.

(Pause)

Your higher self beams... with light.
You feel the pureness of your soul... and you see the inner truth... and beauty of others.

(Pause)

Your pure interactions with others flows... and this benefits all.
See these pure interactions spread around the world.
All worries lift... as people feel connected to their pure inner truth.
Worries lifting... all around the world... as people see the true essence of all.

Such a peaceful feeling... feeling the true connection of your soul.

The energy on the Earth feels so light... all the Earths tensions have lifted.
The Earth looks lighter... its energy field is clear.
See the Earth sparkle... so clear... so peaceful.

(Pause)

The Earth is so special to you... and you rest for a moment in that special place in nature.
With the earth beneath you... you smell the freshness of the plant life... butterflies flutter around you... feel the breeze brush past your skin... gently stimulating your senses.

Resting.

(Pause)

Feeling well rested... the butterflies circle around you... then flit away.
You take a deep breath... and begin to become aware of your physical body.

COLOURED LOVING RIPPLES

You take a deep breath... as you rest... on the sloping bank...
of the clearest stream.
The air is fresh... and there are beautiful trees all around.
The birds sing in these magnificent trees... as you rest.

(Short Pause)

Resting on the bank... of the clearest stream.
Your hands are resting in your lap... as you hold a beautiful
piece... of rose quartz.
Feel the energy... of this pink crystal.
How does it make you feel... as you hold it in your hands?

(Short Pause)

Connect with this crystal... and heal your body.

(Short Pause)

The stream you are sitting near... is so clear... you can see the
bottom.
On the bottom of this stream are crystals... in all different
colours.

(Short Pause)

The water is both healing... and full of loving energy.

You look along the bank.

Beside you... and on the other side of the stream... are other
people.
They too have rose quartz crystals in their hands.

You spend a few moments considering the significances of the
rose quartz crystal... and then gently throw this beautiful
crystal into the calm, clear stream.
You immediately notice the coloured, loving ripples spread
throughout the stream.

You watch as the ripples spread throughout the water.

(Short Pause)

The other people along the bank... also gently throw their rose quartz crystals into the stream.
And immediately... coloured, loving ripples... spread throughout the stream.
You watch as the ripples spread throughout the water.

(Pause)

These ripples spread... and the ripples from your crystal... meet with the ripples from the other people's crystal.
You watch with awe as this occurs.
The loving, colourful ripples... continue to spread throughout this clear stream.

(Short Pause)

The ripples reach the other side of the bank of the stream... and lap against the feet of the person sitting there.

The loving, colourful ripples turn... and come back toward you... meeting and lapping at your feet.

Spend a few thoughtful moments on the effects this process has upon you... and all those who sit along this stream.

(Pause)

You are now aware of the benefits this stream has on you.
You are now feeling refreshed... energised... renewed... cleansed... and full of loving energy.

(Long Pause)

Thankful for your experience at the stream... you know it is time to return... you take a deep breath... and become aware of your physical body.

MAGICAL HEALING CARPET

You take a deep breath... as you walk calmly through a green... grassy field... on a beautiful day.
Walking... brushing your feet through the grass... and you feel a gentle breeze on your skin.

(Pause)

As you walk through the grass... you discover a special carpet... that is laid out on the ground.
You step on this carpet... and as you do... it glows the full spectrum of colours.
You sit down on the carpet... and rest.
Resting on this magical healing carpet.

Feel your body begin to re-energise as you rest.

(Short Pause)

Feeling full of vitality... you notice the carpet has started to hover above the ground.
You feel a floating sensation... as the carpet slowly rises in the air.

You feel safe and in control...

Just floating... on this magical, healing carpet... above the trees on this beautiful day.

Resting.

(Pause)

The air is fresh... and the sun is shining.
You feel completely relaxed with the floating feeling... that is filling your body.

Slowly... the carpet continues to rise.

(Pause)

The trees look very small now.
The carpet continues to rise... and you look down upon the Earth.

(Short Pause)

The carpet begins to move... and before you know it... you are hovering above [insert name of country].
Just resting on this magical healing carpet... above [insert name of county].
The carpet shines... and glows a full spectrum of colours... beginning to sparkle.
As you look at [insert name of country]... the whole country glows a brilliant shade of [insert chosen colour of the rainbow, i.e. violet, indigo, blue, green, yellow, orange and red].
You are amazed at the colour healing occurring in [insert name of country].
You float there for a moment... relaxing... witnessing this beautiful site.

(Pause)

[repeat the bold section several times inserting the name of a different country and colour.]

The magical healing carpet... glows the full spectrum of colours... and begins to lower you to the ground.
Resting you once again... on that green, grassy field.

(Short Pause)

Resting once again... on the green, grassy field... rejuvenating.

(Pause)

Your body is now feeling full of vital energy.
You step off the carpet... onto the green, grassy field.

Walking back the way you came... brushing your feet... through the grass... while the breeze gently brushes over your skin.

(Pause)

Walking through the green, grassy field… walking back the way you came.

You take a deep breath and become aware of your physical body.

LET THE LIGHT IN

Gently breathing in… and out… at your own peaceful pace.

Taking a deep breath.
And in your mind… you open your eyes.

(Short Pause)

Before you, you see… a glorious early morning sun.

(Short Pause)

You sit… on a sandstone cliff-top… comfortable and safe.
Looking out at this early morning sun… experiencing the native bushlands… as the sun shines down and warms your body.

(Short Pause)

The sun shines… the light rays sparkle in the air… and you let the light in.
Breathing in the beautiful, sparkling light rays… as you let the light in.
Letting the light into your body and into your life.

(Short Pause)

You shine like the sparking light rays of the sun… as you have now let the light in.

(Short Pause)

The glorious early morning sunrays sparkle… and you become aware of a glittering in the air.
These sparkles fill the air… as far as you can see.

You are aware of the connectedness of all… as you let the light in.

(Short Pause)

In your mind… you call out.
Call out… to your friends… loved ones… and the rest of
mankind… to breathe in these beautiful, sparkling light rays…
and let the light in.

As you call out… the sun shines brightly on this glorious
morning… and the sun's light rays sparkle intensely in the air.

Your friends… loved ones… and mankind breathe in… and let
the light in.
Letting the light into their physical bodies… and into their
lives.

(Short Pause)

Your friends… loved ones… and mankind… now shine like
the sparking light rays of the sun… as they have now let the
light in.
Aware of the connectedness of all… as they let the light in.

(Short Pause)

The sun shines high in the sky.
It is truly a beautiful day.
In your mind… you gently close your mind's eye.
You take a deep breath in… and become aware of your
physical body.
Taking a deep breath in… becoming aware of your earthly
physical body.

THE DANDELION

You take a deep breath.
And find yourself sitting... in a field.
Just resting in the grass.
So green.

Noticing all the three-leaf clover... as you run your hands through the grass.
You discover a four-leaf clover... which you hold in your hands... a gift for you.
As you do... colours appear around your body... and you feel re-energised.

Feeling like a small child... rejoicing... so happy that you have found a four-leaf clover.

(Short Pause)

Aware of yourself as a child... you concentrate on the sparkling colours around your body.
What colour or colours do you see?
Absorb the colours... take the colours deep within your body and heal.

(Short Pause)

You feel lively... joyful... and full of energy... just like a small child.
You notice the butterflies flittering through the air... and you follow them.
Light as a child... you skip and leap through the clover... following the butterflies.

(Short Pause)

As you follow the butterflies... you come to an inviting patch of grass... with flowers that are special to you as a child. Snapdragons... dandelions... and daisies.

You squeeze the snapdragons and make them talk... having so much fun.

(Short Pause)

You notice a dandelion... that has gone to seed.
Maybe you had a special name for them when you were a child?

Such a long stalk... with so many seeds.
Full of potential... waiting to be blown... so the seeds of potential can grow.

You pick the dandelion ever so gently... and as you do, the dandelion changes colour... a bright colour.
Colours dart around your body... and you are full of excitement for the future.
A pure future... full of love and joy.

The seeds of the dandelion are all your hopes and dreams.
You gently blow on the dandelion... and the coloured seeds scatter in the wind... being blown around the world.

Hopes and dreams for the future... full of love and joy.
See the seeds spread... and grow... a gift to the world.

(Short Pause)

Sitting in the grass... on this beautiful day... you decide to make daisy chains and play.

(Long Pause)

Noticing the butterflies that are flittering through the air... you follow them back... skipping and leaping.
The butterflies lead you back to the grassy area of clover... where you found your four-leaf clover.

(Short Pause)

This joyful child you rediscovered today… is always within you… and you may come back to this field at any time you wish.

You hold the four-leaf clover in your hand and take it with you as you leave.

FEATHER FROM GREAT SPIRIT

Taking a deep breath.
Sitting on a mountaintop.
Resting peacefully... against a large... earthy boulder.
The air is so fresh... and crisp.

The sun shines and your body relaxes... with the warm rays of
light.
You notice tiny sparkling lights in the air... and a feather gently
floats down through the air... and lands in your lap.
You look up and see a bird circling high up in the sky... and
you know that this is a message from Great Spirit.
Take a moment... with your feather... and receive your
message.

(Pause)

The boulder that you are leaning against is so earthy... it
relieves any tensions in your body.
Feeling relaxed and free of tension... you hold your feather in
your hand and gaze at it.
Connecting with it.

(Short Pause)

You begin to run your fingers along the feather... as you do...
the tiny sparkling lights in the air... intensify.

An intense light shines above your head.
This light shines... filling your body and surrounding it in light.

Your body begins to buzz with energy.
The light expands from your body... out into your aura.
So vibrant.
Connected with this glorious light... full of universal love.

(Short Pause)

Still holding your feather from Great Spirit... with both your hands.

You gently blow on it... bringing your attention to the feather... and the world that you are a part of.

Breathing universal love through this feather... out into the world... for all those in need.

(Short Pause)

You see the tiny sparkling lights... spread and float through the air to all those in need as you breathe through the feather.

(Short Pause)

See the tiny sparkling lights intensify... as they reach all those in need... delivering universal love.

(Pause)

Gently blowing on the feather... breathing universal love through the feather... and out into the world.

(Pause)

You thank Great Spirit for the feather... and the healing... as you rest peacefully against the large, earthy boulder on the mountaintop.

(Pause)

Resting peacefully... against the large earthy boulder on the mountaintop...

You take a deep breath... and become aware of your physical body.

Taking a deep breath... aware of your earthly, physical body.

THE FEATHER OF PEACE AND HEALING

Taking a deep breath.
Sitting... on the top of a mountain.
Breathing in... the beautiful... crisp... clean air.
Looking out... at all the beautiful scenery.

The air is so crisp... clean... and fresh.
The sky is magnificent.
There is a slight breeze.
Feel the cool... crisp... invigorating breeze... circulate all around your body.

(Short Pause)

The breeze circulates around your body... in a spiral fashion.
Spiralling around your head... face... and body.
This invigorating breeze makes your body tingle... and buzz with energy.

The tingling energy increases... and a white feather floats down... amongst the spiralling breeze.
This feather brings healing energy to you... and is a message from Great Spirit.
Reminding you of your potential... and how much you are loved.

(Short Pause)

Another white feather appears in the breeze... spiralling around your body... then another... and another... until you are surrounded by white feathers.
They spiral around your body... as they float in the breeze.
Such a beautiful sight.

(Short Pause)

The tingling around your body… and against your skin… has increased tenfold.
Some of these feathers have landed on your body.
Notice… where these feathers… have landed on your body.
They have landed on your body… to heal you.

(Short Pause)

Absorb this magnificent healing… deep within you body… knowing that this healing comes from the most pure source.
Love.

(Short Pause)

The other feathers are floating in the breeze… spiralling around your body.
The breeze stands still… and so do the feathers.
They have stopped circulating around your body… and now float motionless… in mid-air.

You reach out your hands for one of the feathers.
You stroke this feather… connecting with it.

(Short Pause)

As you do… a name of a country… friend… or loved one… comes to mind.
Send this feather… which is full of healing energy… there now.
You let the feather fall from your hands… and it floats to the country… friend… or loved one.
Delivering peace… and healing.

(Short Pause)

You reach out your hands… for one of the feathers.
You stroke this feather… connecting with it.

(Short Pause)

As you do… a particular type of animal comes to mind.
Send this feather… which is full of healing energy… to that particular type of animal now.
You let the feather fall from your hands… and it floats to the animals… delivering peace… and healing.

You reach out your hands... and place a particularly large white feather... on your heart centre.

You hold it there... with both your hands... with your eyes... gently closed.
You feel peaceful.
You connect with your soul... you connect with love.

(Short Pause)

Ever so gently... you breathe out... and in your mind's eye... you open your eyes to see all the feathers floating out into the world... to spread peace... love... and healing.
These healing feathers... reach all those in need.

(Long Pause)

In your hands... you hold the magnificent, large white feather... against your heart centre.
This feather is a gift for you... from Great Spirit.
You say thank you... for the feather... and take a deep breath.
You become aware of your physical body.
Breathing deeply... becoming aware of your earthly, physical body.

GRAIN OF SAND

Breathing deeply.
Breathing in the beautiful light rays of the sun.

(Short Pause)

Breathing in... the beautiful light rays of the sun... deep into
your body.
Relaxing your body.
Breathing in... the beautiful light rays of the sun... deep into
your body.
Letting your muscles relax.
Letting your whole body... relax.

The sun shines brightly... as you breath in deeply.
You find yourself resting... on a pristine white beach.

(Short Pause)

You feel the sand between your fingers... and toes... as you lie
resting... on the beach.
The sun warms your body... as it gently shines down upon
you.
You move your arms... and legs... through the sand... as you
rest on the beach.
Settling your body... into the warm sand.
Relaxing.

(Short Pause)

Relaxing in the warm sand... with your toes pointing towards
the waves of the ocean.
You can hear the gentle sounds... of the waves in the
background.
Your body relaxes... more... and more.

(Short Pause)

Any tension in your body… is released.
Released through the soles of your feet.
Drawn out… through your grounding chakra… below your feet.

(Short Pause)

Drawn out… into the ocean… as you breathe in… the healing light rays… from the sun.
Breathing in the beautiful light rays of the sun.
Releasing any tension… through your feet… through your grounding chakra… into the ocean.

Releasing.

Your body is so relaxed… resting in the sand.
The sand on the beach… is pristine white… in colour.
So many grains of sand.
Grains of sand… surrounding… and supporting your body.

So many grains of sand… making up the whole of the beautiful beach.
Your body rests gently… in the sand.
Part of the beach.
You become the sand… grains of sand.
Part of the beach.

Experiencing the oneness.

(Pause)

You hear the sound of the ocean.
The gentle sounds… of all those waves.
They call… and speak to you… as they wash in… and out.

You have become one with the beach.

Experiencing the oneness… as you feel your body as part of the beach.
Part of the sand.

(Short Pause)

You feel the warmth of the sand... as the sun shines down on you.

One with the sand... making up the whole.

One with everything.

Overcoming obstacles... one.
Bathe in your experience... of oneness... with the universe.

Listening to the ocean waves.

(Short Pause)

Absorbing the sun's light rays... that shine down upon you.

(Short Pause)

Feeling the breeze... that rushes past you.

(Short Pause)

Grains of sand.
One... with it all.

(Short Pause)

Feel the connection... the union.
One.

Peace.

One.

The sun shines down on your body... as it once again rests on the sand.
You wriggle you fingers and toes in the sand... as you lay resting on the beach.

(Short Pause)

Taking a deep breath... you bring your attention back to your physical body.
Breathing deeply... bringing your attention to your earthly, physical body.

THE CLOUD OF COLOUR

Taking a deep breath... as you rest in the lush... green grass... on this beautiful day.

Lying in the lush... green grass... as you look up at the fluffy clouds in the sky.

Just relaxing... on this beautiful day.

Aware of the smell... of the lush... green grass... that you're lying in.

Feeling the connection that you have with the Earth.

(Short Pause)

Feel the energy from the Earth... fill your body... as you lie in the lush... green grass.

Simply resting your body... as you watch the clouds.

(Short Pause)

The clouds change shape... and a beautiful Light Being... appears in front of you... as a rainbow appears... filling the whole sky.

You feel lighter... and your body begins to float... as you become relaxed.

(Short Pause)

Your whole body... now floats in the air... under the presence of this beautiful rainbow... that fills the sky.

You rest upon one of the many fluffy, white clouds.

So comfortable... and so soft.

Just resting... on a white, fluffy cloud.

(Short Pause)

Relaxing more… and more… as the healing colours from the rainbow… filter through the cloud… and fill your body… as you rest.

Glorious red… orange… yellow… green… blue… indigo… and violet… fill the sky.

(Short Pause)

You reach a deep state of relaxation… as the cloud is made up of universal healing light.

Resting… and relaxing… in this beautiful white, fluffy cloud… under the presence of the rainbow.

See the [insert one of the colours of the rainbow eg. red] light ray… of the rainbow… gently shower down upon you… filling every aspect of your body.
The colour [insert the same colour as above eg. red]… from the beautiful rainbow… heals and balances your body and your being.
See the cloud turn [insert the colour as above eg. red]… as your body absorbs the healing colour.
Healing… as you rest… and relax… as you float on this special cloud.

(Short Pause)

The cloud begins to float… across the land… spreading healing light… from the [insert colour as above eg. red] light ray… as you enjoy the view.
The cloud floats across the land… spreading the [insert colour as above eg. red] healing light.
Healing.
The colour fades… and the cloud is motionless.

(Short Pause)

[repeat the bold section seven times, inserting a different colour of the rainbow each time i.e. red, orange, yellow, green, blue, indigo, violet]

The cloud... ever so slowly... begins to lower to the ground. Leaving you resting... upon the lush... green grass. The cloud returns to its rightful place... as it gently begins to rain.

(Short Pause)

And you become aware... of your connection to the Earth... as you feel the grounding energy... of the Earth fill your body. Smelling the fresh... green grass. You take a deep breath... as you become aware of your physical body. Breathing deeply... aware of your earthly, physical body.

RAINBOW HEALING

Breathing deeply… as you picture a large, beautiful tree… with lots of green grass surrounding it.
The tree is very large… and very old.

You sit on the grass… with your back leaning up against the tree.
You continue to breathe deeply.

(Pause)

Here you can let go of any tensions… and any worries.
Just letting go… with the assistance of this beautiful tree.

Sitting on the grass… leaning against the tree.
You become aware… of your connection with the Earth.
Feel the ground beneath you.
Feel the loving energy… from the Earth Mother… flow up through your feet.

Aware of your connection with the Earth… the Earth energy flows up through your feet… through your legs… up to your torso… up to your neck… and shoulders.
Spreading along your arms… and up to your head.
Feel this earth energy… spread around your whole body.

(Pause)

Totally filled… with this loving energy.
Feeling grounded and relaxed.

Sitting on the grass… with your back leaning up against the tree.
You continue to breathe deeply.

(Pause)

Feeling relaxed... you notice the rainbow in the sky.
Beautiful colours... up in the sky.
You open your hands... and the rainbow travels from the sky... into your hands.

(Pause)

In your opened hands... you hold a beautiful rainbow... with beautiful, healing light rays.
The rainbow stretches... from the palm of one hand... to the other.
You sit and focus... on the rainbow... and connect with it deeply.

(Pause)

You now focus... on the [insert a colour i.e. violet, indigo, blue, green, yellow, orange and red]... light ray... of the rainbow.

Let the [insert a colour i.e. violet, indigo, blue, green, yellow, orange and red]... light ray... of the rainbow... flow through your body... absorbing the healing... that is right for you.

(Pause)

Allow the [insert a colour i.e. violet, indigo, blue, green, yellow, orange and red]... light ray... of the rainbow... flow into the Earth... deep into the Earth... healing the Earth.

(Pause)

Allowing the Earth to absorb what it needs.

Now see the [insert a colour i.e. violet, indigo, blue, green, yellow, orange and red]... light ray... of the rainbow... spread around the Earth... to all the plants... animals... and people that require healing.
Allow the plants... animals... and people... to absorb the healing... that is right for them... from the [insert a colour i.e. violet, indigo, blue, green, yellow, orange and red]... light ray of the rainbow.

110

(Pause)

In your hands... you hold a beautiful rainbow... with beautiful, healing... light rays.
The rainbow stretches... from the palm of one hand... to the other.

[repeat the bold section seven times inserting a different colour each time i.e. violet then indigo, blue, green, yellow, orange and red.]

Now see the rainbow's light rays... surrounding you.
Glowing with the many colours... of the rainbow.

(Pause)

You lift your hands... and the rainbow travels back into the sky.

(Pause)

Still sitting on the grass... leaning against the tree.
You once again become aware... of your connection with the Earth.
Feel the ground beneath you.
Feel the loving energy... from the Earth Mother... flow up through your feet.

Aware of your connection with the Earth... the Earth energy flows up through your feet... through your legs... up to your torso... up to your neck... and shoulders.
Spreading along your arms... and up to your head.
Feel this earth energy... spread around your whole body.

(Pause)

Totally filled... with this loving energy.
Feeling grounded... and relaxed... you breathe deeply.

ATMOSPHERIC CLEANSING CLOUD

You take a deep breath... and look up to the sky.
You see the most wonderful white, fluffy cloud... that seems to have a face in it.
The breeze blows gently... from this cloud.
Brushing past your skin... cleansing and invigorating your aura.
Any negativity is swept up into this cleansing cloud.
Leaving your aura clear... clean... and sparkling.

The breeze continues to blow gently... from this cloud.
You can see the energy of the breeze... as it blows... cleansing.

You focus now... on the air and atmosphere... of the Town you live in.
See the breeze blow... from this special cloud.
Gently blowing.
The cloud sweeps away any pollution.
Sweeping away pollution... from the Town you live in... drawing it up into this cloud.
Any pollution... is now swept up into this cleansing cloud.
Leaving the air and atmosphere... of the Town you live in... clear... clean... and sparkling.

(Pause)

The breeze continues to blow gently... from this cloud.
You can see the energy of the breeze... as it blows... cleansing.

You focus now... on the air and atmosphere... of the State you live in.
See the breeze blow... from this special cloud.
Gently blowing.
The cloud sweeps away any pollution.
Sweeping away pollution... from the State you live in... drawing it up into this cloud.

Any pollution... is now swept up into this cleansing cloud.
Leaving the air and atmosphere... of the State you live in...
clear... clean... and sparkling.

(Pause)

The breeze continues to blow gently... from this cloud.
You can see the energy of the breeze... as it blows... cleansing.

You focus now... on the air and atmosphere... of the Country
you live in.
See the breeze blow... from the special cloud.
Gently blowing.
The cloud sweeps away any pollution.
Sweeping away pollution... from the Country you live in...
drawing it up into this cloud.
Any pollution... is now swept up into this cleansing cloud.
Leaving the air and atmosphere... of the Country you live in...
clear... clean... and sparkling.

(Pause)

The breeze continues to blow gently... from this cloud.
You can see the energy of the breeze... as it blows... cleansing.

You focus now... on the air and atmosphere... of the whole
planet.
See the breeze blow... from the special cloud.
Gently blowing.
The cloud sweeps away any pollution.
Sweeping away pollution... from the whole planet... drawing it
up into this cloud.
Any pollution... is now swept up into this cleansing cloud.
Leaving the air and atmosphere... of the whole planet...
clear... clean... and sparkling.

(Pause)

Now see the cloud... the wonderful white, fluffy cloud.
You take a deep breath... and look up in the sky... and see the
cloud surrounded by a rainbow.

(Short Pause)

See the face in the cloud smile... as the pollution disappears into the light... and is replaced with cleansing energy... from the rainbow.

(Short Pause)

It now... gently... begins to rain.

(Pause)

You smile as it rains... and you become aware of your physical body.

HEALING BALLOONS

You take a deep breath.
Sitting... resting... breathing... as you sit under a magnificent tree.
Sitting... resting... breathing... with your back against the magnificent tree.
Sitting... resting... breathing... while rainbow colours surround you... and the magnificent tree.
Sitting... resting... breathing... allowing the beautiful rainbow colours... into your body.
And as you breathe... you absorb the beautiful rainbow colours... as they glisten and shine around your body.

(Pause)

There is such a beautiful and tranquil feeling here.

(Pause)

In front of you... you see a gathering of beautiful spiritual beings... that come to you with pure loving intentions.
Each spiritual being stands before you... quietly... and ever so peacefully.
Each holding a colourful balloon.
The balloons are filled with healing light energies.
And each balloon... is a different colour.

You watch with respect... as the beautiful spiritual beings... stand gathered before you.
Quietly... and peacefully... one of the spiritual beings steps forward... and stands directly in front of you... holding a colourful healing balloon... while you rest there at the tree.
You gaze at each other with love... and you are filled with peace.

(Short Pause)

Communicating with each other... you discuss the healing properties the balloon holds... as it is given to you... to heal your heart.
You receive the healing... and bloom.

(Short Pause)

The being shimmers away.

(Short Pause)

Quietly... and peacefully... another one of the spiritual beings steps forward... and stands directly in front of you... holding a colourful, healing balloon... while you rest there at the tree.
You gaze at each other with love... and you are filled with peace.

(Short Pause)

Communicating with each other... you discuss the healing properties that the balloon holds... and who it is for.

(Short Pause)

Maybe it is for you... maybe a friend... a loved one... or perhaps a stranger in need.
Joined with your pure love... the spiritual being shimmers away... to deliver the healing balloon... to where it is needed.

(Pause)

Quietly... and peacefully... another one of the spiritual beings steps forward... and stands directly in front of you... holding a colourful healing balloon... while you rest there at the tree.
You gaze at each other with love... and you are filled with peace.

(Short Pause)

Communicating with each other... you discuss the healing properties that the balloon holds... and who it is for.

(Short Pause)

Maybe it is for you... maybe a friend... a loved one... or perhaps a stranger in need.
Joined with your pure love... the spiritual being shimmers away... to deliver the healing balloon... to where it is needed.

(Pause)

One by one... the beautiful spiritual beings... continue to step forward... with their coloured healing balloons.
Each discussing the healing properties that the balloons hold... and who they are for.

Joined with your pure love... the spiritual beings shimmer away... to deliver the healing balloons... to where they are needed.

(Long Pause)

As the healing balloons are delivered to where they are needed... you are thanked... and blessed by the universe.

The sun shines down on you... as you sit... rest... and breathe... beneath the magnificent tree.

The sun shines down... warming your body.
Your body is filled with glorious sunshine.
Sitting... resting... breathing... as you sit under the magnificent tree.

SENDING LOVE TO WATER

A bright light shines above you... and beautiful energy droplets flow down from this beautiful, peaceful light... from high above.
You feel love... the purest kind.
Love for you.
Love for our planet... and love for the precious water... that the planet is blessed with.
In your own very special way... you can send love to the water in our planet.

(Pause)

We send love in our own very special way... to the streams in our towns and cities... all around the world.
We send love now.

(Short Pause)

See the streams perfectly balanced now.
Within the universal laws... and in accordance with the highest good.

(Pause)

We send love in our own very special way... to the waterfalls all around the world.
We send love now.

(Short Pause)

See the waterfalls perfectly balanced now.
Within the universal laws... and in accordance with the highest good.

(Pause)

We send love in our own very special way... to the dams... in all the countries... all around the world.
We send love now.

(Short Pause)

See the dams perfectly balanced now.
Within the universal laws... and in accordance with the highest good.

(Pause)

We send love in our own very special way... to the rivers all around the world.
We send love now.

(Short Pause)

See the rivers perfectly balanced now.
Within the universal laws... and in accordance with the highest good.

(Pause)

We send love in our own very special way... to the lakes all around the world.
We send love now.

(Short Pause)

See the lakes perfectly balanced now.
Within the universal laws... and in accordance with the highest good.

(Pause)

We send love in our own very special way... to the springs and running water... beneath the ground.
We send love now.

(Short Pause)

See the springs and running water... beneath the ground... perfectly balanced now.
Within the universal laws... and in accordance with the highest good.

(Pause)

We send love in our own very special way... to the Arctic... at the North Pole.
We send love now.

See the Arctic at the North Pole... perfectly balanced now.
Within the universal laws... and in accordance with the highest good.

We send love in our own very special way... to the Antarctic at the South Pole.
We send love now.

See the Antarctic at the South Pole... perfectly balanced now.
Within the universal laws... and in accordance with the highest good.

We send love in our own very special way... to the seas and oceans... all around the world.
We send love now.

See the seas and oceans... perfectly balanced now.
Within the universal laws... and in accordance with the highest good.

We send love in our own very special way... to all the water on this planet.
We send love now.

See all the water on this planet... perfectly balanced now.
Within the universal laws... and in accordance with the highest good.

The bright light shines above you... and beautiful energy droplets flow down from this beautiful, peaceful light... from high above.
You feel love... the purest kind.
Love for you.
Love for our planet... and love for the water that the planet is blessed with.

You hear the echoes of thank you.
You smile and breathe deeply.

THE CHAKRA SYSTEM
OF ONENESS

Concentrating on your breath... and what you see before you.
And before you... is oneness... which you are a part of.
Oneness.

(Pause)

The most beautiful light presents itself... streaming down...
right in front of you.
You observe this oneness... from a distance.
Beautiful light streaming down.
A tremendous light beam.

(Pause)

A light beam with gigantic... beautiful flowers along it.
The chakra system of oneness.

(Short Pause)

And you of course... are a part of this oneness.
We are all a part of the oneness.

(Pause)

Once you have realised this... you no longer need to observe
the oneness from a distance.
You merge with the light beam.
Oneness.

Presently... where do you reside... with the oneness?

(Short Pause)

Presently... you may sit with the red petals... of the base
chakra of oneness.

(Short Pause)

You observe who else... presently sits here... with you at the red base chakra flower... of oneness... the petals of the flower.
You breathe in the light... colour... and fragrance of the oneness.
Blooming.
One.

Or maybe you presently reside... with the orange petals... of the sacral chakra of oneness.
You observe who else... presently sits here... with you at the orange sacral flower of oneness... the petals of the flower.
You breathe in the light... colour... and fragrance... of the oneness.
Blooming.
One.

Or maybe you presently reside... with the yellow petals... of the solar plexus chakra of oneness.
You observe who else... presently sits here... with you at the yellow solar plexus flower of oneness... the petals of the flower.
You breathe in the light... colour... and fragrance... of the oneness.
Blooming.
One.

Or maybe you presently reside... with the green petals... of the heart chakra of oneness.
You observe who else... presently sits here... with you at the green heart flower of oneness... the petals of the flower.
You breathe in the light... colour... and fragrance... of the oneness.
Blooming.
One.

Or maybe you presently reside... with the aqua petals... of the throat chakra of oneness.
You observe who else... presently sits here... with you... at the aqua throat flower of oneness... the petals of the flower.
You breathe in the light... colour... and fragrance... of the oneness.
Blooming.

One.

Or maybe you presently reside... with the indigo petals... of the brow chakra of oneness.
You observe who else... presently sits here... with you at the indigo brow chakra flower of oneness... the petals of the flower.
You breathe in the light... colour... and fragrance... of the oneness.
Blooming.
One.

Or maybe you presently reside... with the violet petals... of the crown chakra of oneness.
You observe who else... presently sits here... with you at the violet crown chakra flower of oneness... the petals of the flower.
You breathe in the light... colour... and fragrance... of the oneness.
Blooming.
One.

Oneness... wherever you reside.

(Short Pause)

Reside there... in your truth of your presence... and breathe.

(Pause)

Breathing... as the most beautiful light beam streams down... filling the flowers full of bountiful energy... in the most beautiful forms.
Oneness.

The light swirls... from petal to petal.
And in your own time... you move from flower to flower.

(Long Pause)

Glistening... and shining... you take a deep breath.

BLESSED BLANKETS

You take a deep breath... as you rest in a calm... beautiful...
and safe place in nature.
A special place... your special place in nature... you rest there
now.

You breathe deeply... as you rest in this special place in nature.

(Pause)

In front of you... you find there are two square wrapped
parcels... glowing in white light.
One is addressed to you... the other is addressed to a person in
need.
You may know this other person... or it may be someone you
haven't met.

A white eagle appears as you pick up the parcel... that is
addressed to the other person.
You fly with the eagle with ease... delivering this parcel to the
person who is currently in need.

(Pause)

You walk up to the person in need... and give the parcel to
them.
They unwrap it... and find it is a bundle of colourful, blessed
blankets.
Blessed blankets... all of different colours.

(Pause)

These blankets are infused with colourful healing properties...
of light energy.
Notice which of the coloured blankets the person holds.

The person wraps themself in the blanket... and absorbs the
healing energy.

You leave the pile of colourful, blessed blankets... with the person... and bid them farewell.

You fly with the eagle... through the brilliant blue sky. Returning to your special place in nature.

(Pause)

You rest in your special place in nature.
With gratitude you open the parcel... that is addressed to you.
You unwrap the parcel that is glowing in white light... and find it is a bundle of colourful, blessed blankets.
Blessed blankets... all of different colours.

You hold the pure white, fluffy blanket... from the top of the pile... in your hands... and wrap it around your body.
You instantly feel warm... cosy... nurtured... and safe.

(Pause)

You take note of the healing... you are receiving.
You rest for a while... as you absorb the colourful healing properties... of light energy.

(Pause)

You now hold the violet blanket... from the top of the pile... in your hands... and wrap it around your body.
Notice the different feelings... created by each of the coloured blankets.

(Pause)

You take note of the healing... you are receiving.
You rest for a while... as you absorb the colourful healing properties... of light energy.

(Pause)

You now hold the indigo blanket... from the top of the pile... in your hands... and wrap it around your body.
Notice the different feelings... created by each of the coloured blankets.

(Pause)

You take note of the healing... you are receiving.
You rest for a while... as you absorb the colourful healing properties... of light energy.

(Pause)

You now hold the blue blanket... from the top of the pile... in your hands... and wrap it around your body.
Notice the different feelings... created by each of the coloured blankets.

(Pause)

You take note of the healing... you are receiving.
You rest for a while... as you absorb the colourful healing properties... of light energy.

(Pause)

You now hold the green blanket... from the top of the pile... in your hands... and wrap it around your body.
Notice the different feelings... created by each of the coloured blankets.

(Pause)

You take note of the healing... you are receiving.
You rest for a while... as you absorb the colourful healing properties... of light energy.

(Pause)

You now hold the yellow blanket... from the top of the pile... in your hands... and wrap it around your body.
Notice the different feelings... created by each of the coloured blankets.

(Pause)

You take note of the healing... you are receiving.
You rest for a while... as you absorb the colourful healing properties... of light energy.

(Pause)

You now hold the orange blanket... from the top of the pile... in your hands... and wrap it around your body.
Notice the different feelings... created by each of the coloured blankets.

(Pause)

You take note of the healing... you are receiving.
You rest for a while... as you absorb the colourful healing properties... of light energy.

(Pause)

You now hold the red blanket... from the top of the pile... in your hands... and wrap it around your body.
Notice the different feelings... created by each of the coloured blankets.

(Pause)

You take note of the healing... you are receiving.
You rest for a while... as you absorb the colourful healing properties... of light energy.

(Pause)

Now surrounded... in white light... you notice the white eagle circling above.
Pleased with the healing... that has just taken place... you take several deep breaths.
Relaxed... and rejuvenated... you breathe deeply.

SEASONS

As you breathe... you connect with the oneness.
Oneness... with the universe.
Oneness... with the seasons.

One with the seasons... one with nature.

(Pause)

Breathing in... the energy... of the sunshine.

(Pause)

Breathing in... the energy... of the moonlight.

(Pause)

Breathing in... the energy... of the raindrops.

(Pause)

Breathing in... the energy... of the snowflakes.

(Pause)

Breathing in... the energy... of the wind.

(Pause)

Just breathing.
Connecting with the oneness.
Oneness with the universe.

Breathing deeply... in... and out.

(Pause)

Feel oneness with the seasons.
The colour sunlight yellow surrounds you at this time... and you absorb what you need... as you breathe in the essence of spring.

Breathing deeply... you become one with the season spring.
Feel your body begin to warm... with spring.

Your body fills with energy.

(Pause)

The warmth penetrates the ground.
Seeds germinate.
Flowers bloom.
There is a lightness in the air.

(Pause)

You hear the sounds of the birds... as they nest... and make
their homes.

(Short Pause)

Feeling energised... with the essence of spring.
Breathing in... you become one... with the energy of spring.
Bathe in this energy... the essence of spring.

(Pause)

The air fills with glittering silver... and golden-coloured
sparkles... and the season changes.

(Short Pause)

The colour rose pink surrounds you at this time... and you
absorb what you need... as you breathe in the essence of
summer.

You breathe in deeply... as the sun shines down.
The intense warmth of the sun... washes over you... as you
breathe in the essence of summer.

Breathing deeply... you become one with the season summer.

(Pause)

Your metabolism activates... with the energy of summer.

You visualise the warming energy of summer... as it moves
through the air... and gently brushes against your skin.
Invigorating your body... mind and spirit.

You feel full of energy... and activity... with the essence of summer.
Breathing in... you become one with the energy of summer.
Bathe in this energy... the essence of summer.

(Pause)

The air fills with glittering silver... and golden-coloured sparkles... and the season changes.

(Short Pause)

The colour green surrounds you at this time... and you absorb what you need... as you breathe in the essence of autumn.

The wind blows... and the air temperature becomes slightly cooler.
Browns... yellows... and oranges abound among the plant life.

(Pause)

You breathe in the essence of autumn.
Breathing deeply you become one with the season autumn.

(Pause)

You watch the leaves... ever so gently fall from the trees.
Releasing... and letting go with ease.
The leaves float through the air... and gently land upon the ground.
You listen... as the autumn leaves... crunch beneath your feet.

You watch... as the wind gently blows.
Leaves circle... and spin through the air.
A spectacular movement of browns... yellows and oranges.
Releasing... and letting go... with the essence of autumn.

Breathing in... you become one with the energy of autumn.
Bathe in this energy... the essence of autumn.

(Pause)

The air fills with glittering silver... and golden-coloured sparkles... and the season changes.

(Short Pause)

The colour red surrounds you at this time... and you absorb what you need... as you breathe in the essence of winter.

You breathe in deeply... as the temperature drops.
Colours deepen.
Coolness abounds... and the air becomes crisp.
As you breathe in the essence of winter.

You breathe in the essence of winter.
Breathing deeply... you become one with the season winter.

(Short Pause)

Ice appears... and life's vigour slows.
Reserving your energy... with the essence of winter.

It begins to snow.
Soft... frosty ice crystals... float and drift through the air.
Clearing... and refreshing... the energy of life.

(Pause)

An uplifting lightness appears... with the presence of the snow.
Feeling refreshed... cleansed... and clear... with the essence of winter.
You breathe in... and become one with the energy of winter.
Bathe... in the energy of winter.

(Pause)

The air fills with glittering silver... and golden-coloured sparkles... and the season continues to change... and so do you.

(Short Pause)

One... with the cycle of the seasons.

CLEANSING WITH THE SEA

Taking a deep breath as you visualise... blue.

Swirls of gentle blue.
Sea blue... gently swirling.
The sea.
Pure.

(Pause)

Water... ever so gently... swirling.
Cleansing.
Detoxifying.
Purifying your body.
Pure.

(Pause)

In tune with the sea... and the power of water.

(Pause)

Swirls of gentle blue.
Sea blue... gently swirling.
The sea.
Pure.

(Pause)

The Goddess of the sea... brings you a clear message.
You spend some time gently communicating... with the
Goddess of the sea.

(Pause)

Concentrating on the sea now.
Visualising the sea... gently being cleansed.
Cleansing.
Detoxifying.
Purifying.
Pure... and calm.

Fresh.
Cleansed.
Pure and sparkling... free from pollutants.

(Pause)

The sea life flourishes.
Spend some time in this magnificent body of water... exploring the sea... and the life within it.

(Pause)

Enjoy your time in this magnificent body of water.

(Pause)

You rise to the surface of the sea now... and with an angelic being's assistance... you float above the sea.

(Pause)

Floating above the sea.

The angelic being takes your hand... and together you polish and strengthen the sea's energetic, protective layer... sending healing energy into... and around... this magnificent body of water.

(Long Pause)

Polishing and strengthening the sea's energetic protective layer... sending healing energy into... and around... this magnificent body of water.

(Pause)

The angelic being is pleased and grateful for all your efforts... and with a gentle wave from the angelic being and the sea... you say farewell.

(Pause)

You breathe deeply... as you say farewell and become aware of your physical body.

THE CANOE AND
THE CRESCENT MOON

Resting...

Laying back in your canoe.

The crescent Moon shines down on you... as you look up at the heavens.

(Pause)

Resting...

Regaining your strength.

(Short Pause)

The breeze blows fresh air... ever so gently... and your canoe glides forward... as you rest... taking in the night air.

(Long Pause)

Rested... you sit in your canoe and take in the glory of this magical evening... that is all around you.

Water lilies float on this vast body of water... and you move the awes of the canoe and glide forward on your journey... to share your love and your knowledge with others.

(Spoken Softly)

Blessing beeth unto you.

Your heart centre opens... and you find the balance of giving and receiving... as the crescent Moon shines down on you.

(Pause)

Feeling the night air on your arms... you breathe in... and let the magic in.

(Pause)

Finding your balance… as you breathe.

Breathing… as you glide forward… across this vast body of water.

Stronger now than you were before.

(Pause)

The crescent moon shines down on you… and in the distance you see kind hearted souls in the light of the shore… at the entrance of the forest.

(Short Pause)

You arrive at your destination.

Your canoe glides effortlessly onto the shore.

You step out of the canoe and are embraced by the arms of the kind hearted.

(Pause)

You are Home.

(Short Pause)

You breathe deeply.

REFERENCES

Jan Thomas, *Chiron Healing®, Cherionia Pty Ltd*, www.cheirionia.com.au

Larraine Crawshaw, *Chariclo Pty Ltd*, www.chariclo.com

Ian White, *Australian Bush Flower Essences*, Bush Biotherapies Pty Ltd, 45 Booralie Road, Terry Hills, NSW. 2084 Australia. www.ausflowers.com.au

OTHER TITLES OF INTEREST
EARTH HEALING MEDITATION
CD SERIES

Atmospheric Cleansing Cloud - CD

Let the Light In - CD

Land Care In Australia - CD

All of the CD's titles above are available for purchase from www.thefloatinglily.com.au

A wide range of meditation downloads are also available from www.thefloatinglily.com.au or by searching Helen Joy Buck on iTunes.